Student Diversity

*Addressing the needs
of all learners in
inclusive classrooms*

FAYE BROWNLIE

CATHERINE FENIAK

Pembroke Publishers Limited

Dedicated to Gaby, who taught us it is possible to keep happy and
healthy and write a book with the help of a preschooler.
And to Karen for looking after Faye.

©1998   Pembroke Publishers
538 Hood Road
Markham, Ontario, Canada L3R 3K9
1-800-997-9807

Distributed in the U.S. by Stenhouse Publishers
431 York Street,
York, Maine 03909
1-800-988-9812

Canadian Cataloguing in Publication Data

Brownlie, Faye
    Student diversity: activities & strategies to support needs in
inclusive classrooms

Includes bibliographical references and index.
ISBN 1-55138-101-X

1. Inclusive education.   I. Feniak, Catherine.   II. Title.

LC1200.B76 1998   371.9   C98-931629-7

Pembroke gratefully acknowledges the support of the Department of
Canadian Heritage.

Editor:	Alan Simpson
Cover Design:	John Zehethofer
Cover Photography:	Ajay Photographics
Typesetting:	Jay Tee Graphics Ltd.

Printed and bound in Canada
9 8 7 6 5 4 3 2 1

Contents

Introduction

Fifteen years ago, we taught segregated special classes in a junior secondary school. One of these classes was even called an "Integrated Class," and the students stayed with the class until their learning goals were achieved. Needless to say, some students spent the term enrolled in the class while others stayed as little as two weeks. Since that time, we have had many different experiences in education. We have tried to create inclusive classrooms and to be more explicit in meeting the learning needs of all of the students in the classrooms we have touched.

Our roles as resource teachers have shifted from an expectation that identified students would have a separate and different program, delivered in a different setting, to a collaborative model wherein the resource teacher and the classroom teacher identify the learning needs of the class and co-plan how best to meet these needs through a differentiated curriculum. The last question to be addressed is where best to deliver the program. Consequently, most of the service delivery now occurs in the regular class with the resource teacher adapting and modifying the curriculum as needed by the learners.

Meeting Student Needs

The demands of today's classrooms include dealing with the increasingly diverse student populations resulting from the inclusion of students with special needs and the influx of large numbers of students who are learning English as a second or third language. As well, curriculums have been rewritten across Canada and the United States to focus on learning outcomes or expectations. Tied to this is a call for criterion-referenced assessment, an assessment focus that includes the students and makes the learning expectations more explicit.

We have long been interested in how to put into practice the best of what we know. Current brain research and learning theory support what intuitive teachers have long known:

- students need to be actively engaged in learning
- students need to belong to a strong community in the classroom
- students need to see themselves as able and capable learners
- students need to set personal learning goals
- students need to be learning in a variety of ways
- students need to be emotionally involved in their learning
- students will learn at different rates
- students need rich, in-depth inquiry
- students learn best when the content is connected to the world and to their lives
- students need choice and clear expectations

Building Vibrant Learning Environments

We invite you into our classrooms to help build vibrant learning environments for all of our students. Each of the scenarios described is situated in a combined or multi-age class, grades 4/5, 5/6 or 6/7. Each of the classes supports full inclusion of learners with special needs and a collaborative resource model. Each of these classes has been affected by a large influx of learners who are learning English as a second or third language. Teachers in each of these classes are trying to make sense of curriculum organized by grade-mandated learning outcomes or expectations, criterion-referenced assessment, and current learning theory. Join us as we attempt to put into practice the best of what we know. Together we can improve learning for all.

1 Support Teachers — A New Look

Stories: The Past

Imagine a combined grades five and six class of twenty-nine students. Of this class, four of the students are levels one and two (just beginning) students for whom English is a second language. Five are identified as level three ESL, one has an SBD (Severe Behaviour Disorder) and is on medication to control his behaviour, one appears to be have an SBD but has not yet been identified, and one student has a learning disability in the area of expressive output. Support is available for these students, largely on a pullout basis, from the ESL teacher, the resource teacher for students with severe learning disabilities, and the school psychologist. Another of the students in the class sees the area counselor weekly. Added to this, the learning assistance teacher supports those students who require short-term intervention. Each of the professionals who support these "special children" is capable and highly supportive of the students and of the classroom teacher. The end result in the classroom, however, is a constantly revolving door; the teacher is left wondering what is actually happening with all of the programming for these students, and what she can do to support their learning in the classroom where they do spend most of their time. Some days, the whole class is together in the classroom for no more than thirty minutes and the class is not at full contractual limit for integration of students with special needs.

Stories: The Present

Return to the same school two years later, and many of these students are now in a combined grades six and seven class. The class composition is similar but the school has changed to a collaborative, noncategorical support model. One resource teacher is assigned to each class, and together the classroom teacher and resource teacher establish a plan of how best to address the learning of the students identified with special needs. The time available for the resource person to work with the classroom teacher is equal to the combined times of the former various support teachers. As well, each team receives two hours of planning time at the beginning of the year to determine their course of action. After that, if more planning time is required, it will be sought out as needed. Some students, especially level-one ESL students, may be pulled out of the classroom for direct instruction from time to time. However, most of the support will occur in the classroom where both the teachers will work with all of the students on their agreed-upon plan. In this classroom, the class is together for the majority of the day.

The Rationale for Inclusion

Inclusion, the movement of students from special classes to regular classes is increasingly popular in North America. This movement affects all teachers, not just the regular classroom teacher. Teachers of special classes or who are nonenrolling teachers and provide support for specific groups of students can include teachers whose students are learning English as a Second Language, severely learning challenged, intellectually challenged, severely behaviour disordered, physically and multiply challenged, culturally diverse, or students who have mild to moderate learning disabilities or communication disorders. Students also have the services of other professionals: counselors, psychologists, speech and language clinicians, aboriginal support teachers, psychiatrists, teachers of the hearing impaired, teachers of the visually impaired, community health nurses, and outreach teachers.

With a support model that is based on aligning specific students with specific teachers, the end result in the classroom is fragmentation. Some of these professionals will always require one-on-one time outside the classroom with specific students. However, we are trying to create a community within the classroom to support learning. All students, including identified students with special needs, are the responsibility of the classroom teacher. As we move to inclusive classrooms that embrace all learners, we must be careful not to exchange special classes for fragmented regular classes. It is critical that we cut down the number of contacts that the classroom teacher has with people whose job it is to support the learning of identified students.

A Description of the Noncategorical Model

In our preferred model of support, the roles of the support teachers are amalgamated into a resource support team. A classroom teacher is assigned one noncategorical resource person. Together these two teachers work out a plan to support the learning of all the identified students with special needs in the classroom. The spillover from this planning and teaching affects many more students — often those grey-area students who are not identified for an Individual Education Plan (IEP) but would benefit from additional teacher time and expertise. The support provided by the resource teacher can occur either inside or outside the classroom, but the plan for support is a collaboration of the two professionals and is curriculum based. Appropriate adaptations and modifications for learners are tied to learners' needs and to grade-level expectations or learning outcomes. The resource teachers meet as a team weekly to consult with one another and to share expertise. They become the link to outside support teams, leaving the classroom teacher free to concentrate on designing effective learning sequences within the classroom.

Viewpoints

Classroom Teacher

For the classroom teacher, this model has much more appeal since together she and her resource person collaboratively plan for the class and adapt and modify the instruction for individual students as needed. The classroom exists as a community and the social aspects of learning are more readily recognized. The classroom teacher is aware of what her students are doing against prescribed learning expectations and can better monitor their progress and their individualized learning plans.

The resource teacher's second set of eyes gives the classroom teacher feedback on the effectiveness of her instruction and where it is that the student's learning breaks down. Support is also instantaneous for these students when the second teacher is in the classroom. For example, the classroom teacher and the resource teacher can co-plan a unit such as Chapter 5, Literature Circles. As the unit unfolds, they adapt the plan to better fit the needs of all the learners. Together they collect evidence of student progress, reteaching concepts when necessary, and moving in different directions when called upon to do so. From this continuous, ongoing classroom assessment and dialogue about student learning and progress, reporting becomes much easier and the teaching becomes more aligned with student need.

Finally, the saying "two heads are better than one" holds true. The collaboration not only provides more direct service to students, but the emphasis on sharing and the opportunity for sharing expertise is foremost.

Resource Teacher

This model needs only a short startup time. Thus the resource teacher can almost immediately begin direct service to students rather than spend inordinate amounts of time in time-tabling, assessment, and individualized (and separate) planning, trying to consult and collaborate with teachers after class.

The planning focus is different. Rather than teaching concepts or skills separate from the curriculum, the resource teacher has the opportunity to work alongside an experienced curriculum specialist, to co-plan how best to adapt these expectations for the special learners. Students do not receive a watered-down version of the regular curriculum. The resource teacher gains a practical understanding of the curriculum and the needs of students, rather than a remedial, diagnostic, or medical model of learning.

There are times when the resource person will want to access the expertise of other members of the resource team. This will occur at weekly meetings, when the resource teachers from the different classes meet to pool their resources and expertise. For example, a former ESL teacher, now in a collaborative resource model, might have specific questions for the former teacher of the students with severe learning disabilities. As we put aside our special titles in this noncategorical model, the territory for special knowledge begins to lose its boundaries.

The focus of this model is on service delivery. Thus the resource teacher is less concerned with labeling and more concerned with addressing the learning needs of students. Most resource teachers have many strategies for adaptation of the curriculum at their fingertips. Being together in the regular classroom provides an opportunity to share these strategies with a larger group of students and the classroom teacher, which extends her effectiveness. Use of these strategies is not specific to labeled students since most students can benefit from more extensive strategic repertoires.

Student

Most intermediate students would prefer not to be removed from their peer group. With this in mind, most of these students recognize that they need the support but would be mortified to be singled out in the classroom to receive one-on-one assistance. It is easier for them if the classroom teacher and the resource teacher are viewed as a team for all the students in the classroom. They are still able to receive the support they require, but it does not need to be fraught with emotional issues. The support is seamless.

Feedback on one's performance toward the learning outcomes of the curriculum is faster. Student performance improves with appropriate, immediate feedback, followed by a chance to practise, both with a coach and independently.

Identification of students in need of support is a less-arduous task. With two teachers present at key times, support is more readily available and the referral process becomes almost nonexistent.

Parents

There should be no more mixed messages. The support person and the classroom teacher are most likely to have aligned their goals for the student if they are engaged in continuous, ongoing, side-by-side teaching. There are fewer people to talk to after reporting and in IEP meetings. Less intimidation should occur, as there will be fewer required meetings of the "full team" with the family.

The Teaching Scenarios in This Book

The teaching scenarios in this book have occurred in schools that embrace this noncategorical model of support delivery. You will notice as you read that there are times when two teachers are working together in the class and other times when the classroom teacher is alone with her students. Most of the delivery of service to students with special needs occurs within the classroom. Rarely are students removed from the class for support. When they are removed, however, the learning expectations and the program have still been co-planned by the teacher and the resource teacher and an alternative setting is deemed to be more beneficial to the student's learning.

2 First Week Considerations

During the first week with a new class of students, we set the tone for the year by involving them in a variety of structured activities, which requires them to:

- meet others in the room
- engage in discussion
- share their findings when reporting back to class
- reflect on their learning and on their participation
- question
- process new information in different ways.

One of the few "rules of the classroom" that we officially share with the students is that the classroom must be a safe place for everyone. Students will not take risks in sharing their ideas and fully participating in activities if they perceive that others will criticize their opinions. They also will not want to engage in group activities if they feel that they are not welcome to join a particular group. It is critical that our classroom becomes a community where all students belong.

Initially, the students are placed into working groups. To do this, we closely observe the students and the communication patterns they exhibit. We also have the students write down the names of two members of the class with whom they would like a chance to work. These lists are collected and, each time we make class groupings, we try to work in some of the requests. Students are guaranteed that, at some point in the year, they will get their first and second choices of group mates.

Much useful information is gained from this quick sociogram. We notice which students are willing to work with any members of the class. These are often students who may be empathetic to students with special educational needs. We do not want them exclusively in groups with students with special needs, but at the beginning of the year they can be students who, with only a little support and coaching, can be peer models of inclusion for the rest of the class. We also take note of which students are most and least frequently listed in the student requests. Many times students want the opportunity to work with another student who is not usually in their social group but who is perceived to be academically strong. These are also students whom we want to enlist as peer models in the development of social skills. The students whose names appear infrequently are carefully placed in groups. We circulate throughout the class during group work, assisting students in the inclusion of all members of the group, in cooperative ways of speaking to each other, and in ways of resolving conflict.

We truly believe in the social aspect of learning and in the students' strong desire to belong. Our personal goal for group work is that by the end of the year, each student in the class can work with any other student in the class, in a way that promotes the learning of all members of the group.

Day 1, Getting Acquainted with a People Search

During the first week, we want activities that will require students to move about the room and speak to each other. On the first day, students work with a People Search (Fogarty, Robin. Thoughtful Cooperative Learning Workshop, Richmond, BC, 1990) in which they must ask their classmates a series of questions in order to discover some of the things that were done over the summer holiday. In this way every member of the class is approached by others and every member must initiate some conversations. The students love finding out about each other's summers. Even the students who are learning English as a second or third language actively participate in this. Once they have heard a question asked, they could use this as a model for approaching others. We are also moving among the students, bridging as necessary to ensure that all are included.

Participating in this **People Search** on the first day alerts the students to the fact that this is a class where talking is expected. As we listen to the noise and notice their smiles, we are reminded of what on-task, engaged, happy students look and sound like. We hope to keep this in mind throughout the year.

Days Two and Three — A Strategic Sequence

Having now established the working groups, we begin with the picture book *A River Ran Wild* by Lynne Cherry (New York: Harcourt Brace, 1992 — about a river endangered by pollution) and work with a connecting strategy, Questioning (B.C. Ministry of Education and Ministry Responsible for Multiculturalism and Human Rights, *Thinking in the Classroom*, Vol. 2. Victoria, BC: B.C. Ministry of Education, 1992). The students are in groups of four. We have chosen three pictures from the text to share with the students, one at a time. While looking at each picture, we ask them to respond to the question "What are you wondering when you see this illustration?" Students take turns in their groups recording their questions. We also ask them to notice the difference in their responses when they are asked to *question* rather than to *tell*. They are simply going to record questions, not answer them at this time. For some, this is a challenge.

After the students have seen all three illustrations, they then decide which of their questions for the first picture is the most creative, for the second is the most thoughtful, and for the third is the most imaginative. We compare these questions as a class; then discuss how we worked together, in groups, to come to a consensus. This gives more information on which social skills to emphasize in the coming weeks.

Next we read *A River Ran Wild* to them. After the reading, the students, in their groups, discuss how their questions matched the author's thinking and how their ideas could have been incorporated into the text.

The following day, we turn to an individual processing strategy, Quadrants, and reread the text. (Brownlie, Faye, Susan Close and Linda Wingren. *Tomorrow's Classroom Today*. Markham ON: Pembroke Publishers, 1990.) While we reread, the students jot down notes and draw images on a piece of paper that has been divided into four boxes labeled Senses, Emotions, Illustrations, and Changes. After the reading, extra time is given so that the students have a chance to record something in each category. They then share their written and pictorial ideas with each other, looking for parallels and differences in their thinking.

A class discussion follows, linking the river in the text to local rivers that are also endangered by pollution. Since B.C. Rivers Day occurs annually at the end of September, the news articles that students bring into class provide local information about the plight of rivers closer to our home. Following these discussions, students write about what they have learned from the text and from the news reports about local rivers.

Summary

These initial strategies have been deliberately chosen because they do not require participation solely through print or relying only on individual response. All of our students are more able to participate if we allow them talk time, some movement, repetition, small-group work, and opportunities to draw and write their thinking before requiring a written response. The specific activities have been chosen because we want to emphasize the community that we are building in our classroom and the links that our curriculum will make to the world outside the classroom. We are now ready to delve more deeply into the mandated curriculum and begin our journey together.

3 Writers Workshop: The Foundation

A Shift in the Teaching of Writing

The writing program is the unifying factor that has links to all that we do in the classroom. It has changed the way we think about planning for teaching, and this has affected the way the students view themselves as learners. It is both powerful and inclusive, as the students' written compositions attest.

The impetus for this change was Nancie Atwell's book, *In the Middle: Writing, Reading and Learning with Adolescents* (Portsmouth, NH: Heinemann, 1987). In this groundbreaking book, Atwell outlines her journey as a teacher of English. She wanted students to be able to write as real authors do rather than writing in response to predetermined topics. Remember the deadly "Write about what you did this summer" topic that was a standard early September assignment?

Nancie Atwell's journey led her to question her assumptions about the way she was teaching writing. Many of her anecdotes about the students she had taught mirrored situations that we had experienced. These were the students for whom writing was not an easy process. It was Atwell's continued reflection on the writing process and how it could be more accessible for all students that informed our practice.

Setting up a classroom for Writers Workshop necessitated a dramatic shift from the teacher as the central figure to the teacher as a facilitator. Essentially, it gave the students the power to determine what they wanted to write about and the genre they would use to reflect their ideas. This incorporated all that we knew about the writing process: brainstorming ideas, writing a first draft, soliciting feedback, revising the draft, editing, proofreading, and finally, publishing. However, it seemed more fluid, perhaps a way of helping students personalize their writing process.

Establishing an Environment for Authors

Initially, we followed Atwell's expertise in planning a classroom that would be conducive to a writers workshop. She outlined some of the shared beliefs that are key to establishing an environment for authors:

- regular time must be devoted to writing
- authors need to choose their own topics
- authors need feedback about their writing
- authors learn the mechanics of writing in the context of their compositions
- authors need to meet other authors
- authors need to read
- teachers of writing need to keep abreast of current research about the craft of writing

To facilitate the activities that are central to the writers workshop period — mini-lesson, status of the class, writing/conferencing and group share — the timetable was adjusted to accommodate one weekly 80-minute block of time and at least two other 40-minute class periods. As the year progressed, the students requested more writers workshop time. Two 80-minute periods per week would have been preferable.

Day One — Getting Students Started

During the initial lesson, writers workshop is described to the students as a time for them to spend on their own writing. They will have an opportunity to write each period. Over the next few weeks of school, the behavioral expectations are further developed and reinforced in mini-lessons. The goal of this first lesson is to get the students started on their first piece of writing.

One way of starting is by telling the students about a personal experience, one with a humorous outcome, which you, the teacher, will write about in writers workshop. This enables the students to see teachers as writers. It also models and reinforces that one's personal experiences are great topics for writing and often result in powerful written compositions. Too often students do not develop as writers because they spend inordinate time writing watered-down television plots.

Once our teacher story descriptions are given, students write or sketch their story ideas. Teachers, too, sit and begin writing. After a few minutes, all are settled into writing down some of their ideas. After about fifteen minutes, students are asked to finish the idea they are writing and reread what they have done. Now is the time for some sharing.

A lead is the initial part of the piece in which the reader decides whether or not the topic is sufficiently engaging to continue reading. This is the point where the topic is introduced and the author's voice is established, making the lead one of the critical points in a composition. Each student identifies her or his lead and then one after another they are asked to read it or to paraphrase their sketches, so the rest of the class can hear the variety of stories being written. It is important that each student is encouraged to participate. From the onset of writers workshop, we want to establish a climate that values each student as a writer with something to say. During the sharing of leads or sketches, no comments are made, other than to make sure each lead can be heard. This activity gives students an equal chance to share some of their writing without the risk of criticism. As well, it allows them to hear various ways to engage an audience. After hearing more than twenty-five selections, they can identify the leads that grabbed their attention. Some writers begin the editing process at this point, without prompting, because they have had a chance to think about ideas that would make their lead more engaging.

Day Two — Introducing the Status of the Class Report

The mini-lesson for the second writers workshop class begins with a rereading of what they have written during the initial period. Students then paraphrase to a neighbour the main ideas in their initial plan for the story. Since most of these are personal experience stories, this is not difficult for the students. After allowing several minutes for discussion, the **Status of the Class Report** is introduced. This is one of the ways a record will be kept of what they are writing. Students are asked to write "Draft 1" at the top of the page of their first story. Each time the story is rewritten, it is recorded numerically with the draft number at the top of the page. These are stored in a writing folder with all of the written work for a term, one folder per student.

As individual students call out their status, they tell the draft number as well as a shortened version of the title or topic for recording. Their progress is then easy to monitor over the term. The response, "Draft 2, Hawaii," indicates that Lindsay is writing her second draft of a personal-experience story of her Hawaiian vacation. Similarly, a student might say, "Draft 1, new." This indicates a new topic, at this time unnamed. Prior to the end of the class, it is wise to have a quick conference with this student and establish a topic. In this way, those writers who may be struggling to begin are not lost in the process. As the term progresses and the students have learned some of the different genres of writing, they respond to the status report by indicating the genre as well as the draft number. If a student requires a conference, she or he indicates this during the status report.

Writers workshop works well for students if they understand the housekeeping chores and do them automatically. These include:

- having a draft number and topic to report (This helps keep a focus.)
- placing all drafts in their writing folders, including those which they choose to discontinue (This helps keep order and traces development.)
- requesting a conference when help is needed (This helps reinforce that you are not in this alone. Writing can be interactive, and some of us require more interaction or reflection to begin. As teachers, our task is to support students' development.)

Students will often change their topics during the first few weeks of writers workshop. As they experiment with capturing their experiences on paper, this is quite a natural process. It is important to monitor carefully the inclusion of all beginning drafts in the portfolio and that, before too long, one draft moves beyond a beginning.

Mini-Lessons

1. Sentence Fluency and Mechanics

The mini-lesson phase of the 80-minute classes is the time when students are taught such topics as paragraphing, sentence structure, punctuation, and other aspects in what we refer to as the "conventions of writing." These lessons are planned based on needs noticed when editing student drafts.

In one of the initial mini-lessons, the students are introduced to the role of teacher as editor. Being an editor allows the teacher to read a student's draft and to record on that draft comments and corrections which might be of assistance to the writer. For each composition, the teacher edits one of the drafts, at some point. As writers, students can choose to disregard the comments, but they are encouraged to read and consider all of the feedback. Sometimes, it is important to have a writing conference with the student, rather than write long editing notes. At this point, the student and teacher can discuss the writing together and the teacher can choose one or two key editing aspects on which to focus. The conferences occur during the class, while other students are writing.

This role of editor is a critical aspect of writers workshop. Editing one draft of each student's composition is highly individualized. The teacher's responses are directed solely by the needs of the student. Differentiation and individualization of the curriculum at this point are automatic. Not only does each student receive feedback that is pertinent to his or her growth as a writer, but the teacher gleans patterns emerging in the writing of the class to enable her to decide which instructional focus to take in the whole-class or small-group mini-lessons.

Jenny is a student who is learning English. She has requested feedback on both drafts of her story "My Trip to Hong Kong." Samples of her writing contain editing notes. Some of these comments have been built together in a conference; the teacher has done some editing, on her own time. As a student learning English, Jenny is working to use past tense verbs correctly and to maintain subject-verb agreement. Her sentence fluency continues to require much 'talk time' as we strive to develop an ear for the rhythm of the English language.

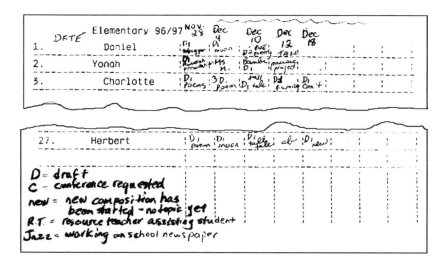

Text Tax

At the beginning of the year much editing focuses on sentence fluency. Many of the authors make errors in sentence construction such as run-on sentences, incomplete sentences, and sentence fragments. A series of mini-lessons teaches the students the components of sentences, sentence combining, and identification of run-on sentences. Published activities and student-generated examples provide a basis for these lessons. **Text Tax** is an activity that involves the students in a small-group editing task.

Text Tax

As the editorial board of our class publication, your job is to read the enclosed text and edit out unnecessary words, Since our government has placed a tax on words ($1.00 per word), editors have been forced to edit carefully to save money. You may not change the author's intended meaning nor drastically alter the effect. You may:

1. Delete unnecessary words or phrases.
2. Substitute words or phrases.
3. Reword a sentence to reduce its length or clarify its meaning.
4. Combine sentences (remember to use the correct linking words).

Please see me for a conference Jenny

Jenny! D! My Trip To Hong Kong In Christmas
1998   Jan 12, 98

    On the Christmas holiday, I went to Hong Kong. I ~~re~~ had to leave before ~~the~~ the day of the actual holiday to catch ~~up the~~ the the plane, because when my parents decided to go to Hong Kong and ~~went~~ *called* to buy tickets, there ~~I~~ *was* only *one* a flight left. *That's why I had* I've to go early one day and come back later a week.

    When I reached Hong Kong, it's *was* at night already. I remember what I did when I got home is that I rushed to open *turn on* the television. The dramas ~~are~~ *are* very good even ~~sp~~ the comercials are good too. Then I went to bed at 12:00 a.m!

    I watched a movie in Hong Kong with my cousins I ~~went to watched~~ *saw* Titanic. ~~It's~~ *which was* a great movie I cried at the end of the movie! ~~The~~ One of my cousins cried out loud. I saw some ~~girls~~ *who* rushed to the washroom to ~~wipe~~ their tears, ~~even there be~~ *There were even* some ~~boys~~ *who were* rubbing their eyes. I loved *the* story R.0.S and also I liked the actors. ~~I~~ *the* One of the ~~actors I~~ *who* liked is Leonardo Di Carprio, in Hong Kong he's very famous, he is m. cousin's idol too.

    Even it *was* only three weeks, but I had a lot of fun, I'm very excited ~~for~~ *about* my Summer holiday!!

[left margin annotations:]
it's = it is

you are writing about events that happened in the past so you'd want to use it was night already

combine these sentences (which was)

past tense verbs: liked / lived R.O.S

Draft 2

Jenny

My Trip To Hong Kong

For
Cap On the 1998 christmas holiday, I went to Hong Kong. I had to leave before the day of the actual holiday to catch the plane, because when my parents decided to go to Hong Kong and called to buy tickets, there was only one flight left. That's why I had to go early one day and come back a week later.

When I reached Hong Kong, it was night already. I remember what I did when I got home is that I rushed to turn on the television. The dramas were very good even the commercial are good too. Then I went to bed at 12:00 am! *↑ plural*

this is part of the previous idea → I watched a movie in Hong Kong with my cousins. I saw Titanic, Which was a great movie. I cried at the end of the movie, And one of my *combine these ideas as 1 sentence* cousins cried out loud. I saw some girls who rushed to the washroom to wipe *ideas as 1 sentence* their tears. There were even some boys who were rubbing their eyes. I loved the story and also I like the actors. One of the actors who I like is Leonardo *ROS →* Di Carprio, in Hong Kong he's very famous and he is my cousin's idol, too!

The only thing I don't like there is the weather and the chicken. *← explain where you are speaking of it* Chicken is my favourite food but because there's a disease called H5N1 in those chickens in Hong Kong, we couldn't eat chicken. I don't like the weather because its cold, very wet and very windy.

My grandpa had a birthday too. All of my cousins, Uncles and Aunties went to a Chinese restaurant for dinner to celebrate.

I brought lots of clothes in Hong Kong because they are very cheap. The next day I went to Hong Kong, I quickly went shopping, I went to six malls!

I went to my Aunty's house to stay over for three days and two nights. The first day, I went to my other Aunty's house for movie for the day. We *something is missing her* bought over $100 for snacks, but we ate all of them. The second day, we went shopping. I bought many things but no clothes. *remember to use past tense*

There are 2 run-on sentences in this part. On my birthday I got an ice-cream cake, its so nice! I got two presents from my cousins, they are a photo frame with Leonardo Di Carprio's picture in it, and a rubbish bin, they said to tidy my room a bit more, I went home on my birthday. *because* *also* Even it was only three weeks, I had a lot of fun. I'm very excited about my summer holiday!!

"Janey, let's go and buy a lottery ticket from the store," I said. Janey is the girl who lives next door. She is my best friend. We went to the store to buy a ticket. When we looked at the numbers we were so excited. We had won! "We've won!" cried Janey. "$10 000!" "Let's go home and tell our parents," I shouted.

2. Introducing Free-Verse Poetry

Writers do not become writers by focusing only on sentence fluency and mechanics. Presenting new genres of writing in mini-lessons enables them to expand their writing repertoire. **Free-Verse Poetry** frees the students to write in a different form and often enables less-able writers.

Distribute magnifiers to pairs of students and take the students on a guided walk around the school, recording signs of autumn as you walk and observe. Prior to this walk, have the students write down the following chart:

Autumn Notes

Sights	Sounds	Smells	Touch	Scientific Information	Other

As they walk, the students record detailed descriptions, phrases, words, and/or pictures in each of the categories. They can wander as a group with the teacher, discussing observations as they go, or they can wander in pairs, observing, comparing, and recording their observations on the chart. The walk takes about fifteen to twenty minutes. Upon returning to the classroom, ask the students to choose a phrase, word, or description of what they had experienced while walking. Record each of these responses on the overhead projector so that the rest of the class can see them. When all the students have added one idea, collect further additions that are not yet represented on the screen. Since these ideas are there for sharing, invite the students to add to their own charts, any particular details that would add to their descriptions, either from the screen or from their own thinking.

Introduce Free-Verse Poetry as a series of words and phrases that can "paint pictures in the readers' minds." Show the students a free-verse poem about autumn or nature or walking as an example of the kind of writing they are going to produce. In the discussion of this poem, draw attention to the imagery and to the lack of rhyme and rhythm patterns that many of the students associate with poetry. The students then work individually to reread their chart, select the ideas they want to express, and write a draft of their autumn poem. By the end of this class, the students submit a number of first drafts for editing. Some of these first drafts contain similes, comparisons that use the words like or as to link two separate objects that have something in common. You can use these student samples of similes to model a literary device for other writers in the class.

Amanda and Lewis provide powerful autumn examples from this experience. Charanpreet also provides a powerful example, focusing on one object that he has seen on his walk. These three students represent the diversity within the classroom.

3. The Group Share Process

Another mini-lesson to present at the beginning of the year is the Group Share Process. Generally, this activity is placed at the end of the writers workshop period. Each author who wants to participate is encouraged to ask the class to focus on a specific aspect of his or her writing, for example, the ending of a story. The student then reads that portion of the composition and asks the class for feedback. Students are taught to respond by providing Praise, Questions, and Suggestions (P.Q.S.). It is important to teach the students to be specific in their responses so that the author receives useful feedback about her/his writing. When students offer praise by saying that they liked the composition because it was funny, they are requested to clarify for the author the parts that are humorous.

Another way to teach students how to give positive feedback is by modeling. Ask the authors of the autumn free-verse poems if their poems can be read anonymously. Read the poems aloud, modeling the P.Q.S. process for the class. In addition to observing how to offer useful feedback, the students also hear a variety of ways to write free-verse poetry, which assists them in writing their own poems. Students are keen to have their writing shared when they realize the sharing is both positive and respectful. For older students, the opinion of their peers is greatly valued.

Autumn — by Amanda

Trees are surprisingly vibrant with shades of red and yellow.
The cool tingling breeze is crisp and fresh.
A light fragrance of dew is in the morning air.
It is autumn.
Leaves gently twirling around to the brown and yellow floor.
The days are short and cool.
Birds are flying south in their orderly fashion.
Trees sway as the wind blows them swiftly.
It is autumn.
I see it.
I smell it.
I hear it.
I feel it.
It is autumn.

Fall — by Lewis

As the leaves fall gracefully to the ground like a ship slowing sinking to the misty ocean floor,
I find that I am one step closer to, but also further away from the summer that
    once was.
As the relaxing fall breeze flows through the street like a silent army
    preparing for battle,
I see the black clouds having all the power of the god called nature.
As the rain starts to slowly fall to the ground like a leaking faucet,
The streets turn to a slippery marsh of leaves.
As the murky water flows to the storm drains,
I taste the first flake of snow as it touches my tongue when this season passes
    once again....

Rock — by Charanpreet

    Staying still like silicon
Little shiny dots like a million pieces of a broken mirror
    Hard like a piece of steel
        Has no home
    Has a life who know's
    Sharp like a knife.

4. Letting Pictures Tell the Story

Teachers have a few stock story ideas for students who are suffering from writer's block. **Letting Pictures Tell the Story** is one of our favourites for students who are lost for a topic.

First, choose six words that will interest your audience, have several possible meanings, and have emotional appeal. The words can also be linked to current curriculum topics. One combination of words that we have used includes *fire, hear/here, youth, anger, confusion, and friendship*. The homonym *here/hear* invites students to think about possible meanings. Words can also relate to a theme like persecution: *escape, hidden, determination, hope, separation*, and *equality*.

Students take a sheet of paper and fold it into six sections. They listen to each word, and then think and draw at the same time the images and associations that come to mind after hearing the word. If many of your students are just learning English, spell out each word to enable them to consult their dictionaries and locate the word. We encourage our students to use their small computers, which allow them to type in an English word and see the corresponding word in their first language and a definition of the word. This support includes ESL students in this activity, while building their English vocabulary.

At the end of one minute, ask the students to stop and then proceed to the next word. This continues until the students have recorded each of the six words. Give them time to discuss their images and ideas with a partner. This will generate a lot of conversation about the similarities and differences in their interpretations of the words. They also enjoy seeing each other's artwork, which varies from stick people to comic book illustrations. For some students, especially those for whom English is another language and those who have language-processing challenges, the opportunity to see how other students visualize the words is especially beneficial. The different meanings depicted in the drawings and associations made by their peers help to develop their vocabularies.

After speaking with a partner, students have several minutes to add any new ideas to their drawings. They then write a narrative composition that includes three or four of the words that were drawn. They can determine which of the word meanings fits best into their story. These stories improve dramatically once students are familiar with the parts of a story — the rising action, conflict, climax, and resolution. Many students find this highly motivating. They want to put the pieces of the literary puzzle together. Some students continue drawing their plan for the story before they begin to write. For them, it is an excellent planning tool to organize the plot of the story in advance. They then have a story ending in mind prior to writing.

Once the class has had ten minutes to write, ask them to pause in their writing and to identify a powerful segment — a phrase or sentence — in their story. Share these; then students continue with writers workshop.

Tiffany and Katannya's samples represent two very different writers who were captured by this way of beginning writing.

Tiffany   **The Vow**   Feb. 14, 1998

It just isn't fair. Nothing's fair. Martin thought sullenly, sitting in detention. *Just becuase I wrote an essay he didn't like, I get detention?* He looked around the room in vain for <u>hope</u> of <u>escape</u>. It was a warm and sunny day, a perfect day to be outside. A teacher, Mr. McKeal, walked in, interrupting his thoughts.

"Hello, Martin. Now what did you do today?"

"Nothing." Martin said defensively. "We were all supposed to write an essay about what we think is important in life, and then read it out loud to the whole class. I wrote about <u>equality</u>, and after I read it out loud, Mr. Green started making stupid suggestions. I got angry and said something, so he sent me here."

Mr. McKeal raised his eyebrows. "Oh really? Mr. Green said you wrote something inappropriate, and he was just trying to help you. Then you started yelling at him."

Martin started to protest, but was cut off by a gesture by Mr. McKeal's hand. "The way I see it, you were being inexcusably rude to your teacher. Although Mr. Green may not have been able to share your point of view, you should have held back your anger. As your punishment, you will write a hundred word essay to apologize to your teacher. Next time, I'd suggest you write something your teacher agrees on. Okay?" When Martin nodded, Mr. McKeal dismissed him.

Frustrated, Martin ran out of the school. *Nobody understands. They're all too narrow-minded.* Taking a deep breath of the fresh autumn air, he made up his mind. Blazing with <u>determination</u>, he made a silent vow. *One day*, he thought, *one day I'll write an essay about what I believe in that they will never, ever forget.*

How Hal the Dog Became Famous   Katannya

"When are we ever going to get out of this kennel?" wondered Hal and his companion. Frankfurt sniffed the air, turned and replied, "Never in our lifetime. This is pound life, hard and unforgiving. You can't stop worrying about what those humans are going to do next. One day you're next to a new dog, the next day you're not. What do they do to them anyway?"

"I guess we can only wait and hope for our turn then," said Hal, lying down and sighing unhappily. The lights in the room flickered off, and sent the whole area into complete darkness. That night a strange figure was entering the room with a flash light. There were footsteps and another figure came into sight. Then there was heavy thumping, and screaming. Hal woke up, startled. A voice started cursing, and then the suspicioius figure left the room quickly. The suspect couldn't see Hal though, because he was hidden in the darkness.

The next day there was a huge commotion. One of the staff had been severely beaten, and was sent to hospital with serious injuries. However, nobody saw or witnessed anything, and the doctor said that the beating had made the victim lose her entire memory. Nobody was a witness...except Hal.

"The dog must have seen everything," said a police officer. "Too bad he can't talk in English."

That day, while a doctor was doing some tests on Hal, he spilt some toxins on him, which immediately sent Hal in a worried frenzy. He tried to bark, but instead, a strange vibration in his throat made a sound like, "ouch!"

Startled, Hal barked again, only to realise that he failed to do so, and only replied "ouch!" again. The doctor fainted right away. Only when he recovered, did Hal speak.

"Hello, I suppose that this may seem strange to you. If you're looking for a witness for the crime, call me anytime," and with that, Hal trotted away through the door.

"Hey, read this," replied a tenant the next day pointing to a newspaper, "pound dog speaks."

"That's amazing!" replied another.

The next day, Hal was summoned to do a tribunal for the beating of the staff member. The suspect sat in a chair, slumped and weary.

"Hal the dog," said the officer. Hal trotted up to the officer, who had to pick him up and put him on the specially laid chair.

"Do you swear to speak the truth and only the truth?" boomed the judge.

"Yes, I do."

"On the night of September the fifth, nineteen eighty nine, there was a beating of a staff member of the local city dog pound. Is that so?"

"Of course," said Hal bluntly.

"Describe the voice that you heard that night of the suspect."

"It was hoarse and he was cursing. His voice was very low and he kept on yelling."

"Thank-you. That will be all." The officer gave Hal a bone as a reward, and Hal took it thankfully.

"The Jury pronounces John McCray guilty of the beating of Sandra Grinder. He is sentenced to twenty years in prison without parol."

And that is how Hal the dog became famous, and became a lawyer.

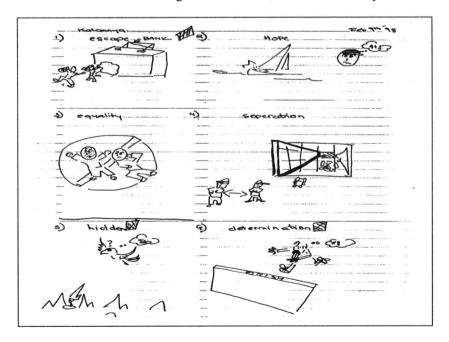

Evaluation

It is important that each author's progress can easily be monitored. This is done in several ways.

1. Status of the Class Check

Record what each of the students is writing each period by doing the Status of the Class Check. At this time, students say if they need to speak to you individually in a conference about their writing. This is either in response to your request, left in your editing notes, or it might be a student's particular concern or question. In scanning the status report for each student over several classes, determine if individual students need a reminder for editing or if they need help in effectively organizing their class writing time. (See the sample on page 24.)

2. Writers Workshop Observations Sheet

Keep a **Writers Workshop Observations Sheet** on each student. (See the sample on page 35.) On this sheet record all of your editing and conferencing notes and the strengths and needs of each author. This is very helpful when writing report cards, because it provides a detailed record of the kinds of writing that have been completed, the writing skills the student has mastered, and the skills that are developing. This sheet flags the students who need help in organizing their writing over a term. For some students, the open-ended nature of writers workshop is a new experience. Typically these students do not use class writing time to their advantage and leave most of their writing to be edited in the last week of the term. This can be prevented by carefully monitoring and requesting conferences about setting goals for completion of drafts. It is also important to have short conferences with all the students about their writing; this sheet provides an overview of the dates of these meetings to ensure that all authors are regularly conferenced.

3. Building Criteria

From time to time we build criteria, as a class, for a specific writing piece. In the Letting Pictures Tell the Story composition, we brainstormed possible ideas for powerful stories and determined which

WRITER'S WORKSHOP
OBSERVATIONS

NAME: Risa   TERM: 1

PERSONAL GOALS FOR MY WRITING: To write a good story or novel with good content and get it $ published

Titles of Edited Drafts   Editing Date
Horse Riding Lesson Draft 1 & 2.   Sept 11
Autumn poem   Sept 26
Voices - thriller.   Sept 28
The Flight   Oct 28
Haikus (3) - autumn   Oct 30

WRITING STRENGTHS
• uses ?ing
• clean narrative
  uses " " to further the plot
• the flight - very descriptive / author like style adapted. Entertaining story.
• poetry contains strong imagry

NEEDS   CONFERENCES
• brackets used rather than including ideas   Sept. 22 conf. about
  in sentences.   explaining horse lingo to
• a few verb tense errors.   non-riders eg giving in her
  elaboration   head'.
• ROS   Oct 28 - conference
• syllables should be used when hyphenating words. decided R. has a problem c
                                              open-ended deadlines - ∴ 1 draft
                                              /wk. in box for me to edit.

WRITER'S WORKSHOP
OBSERVATIONS

NAME: TERM:

PERSONAL GOALS FOR MY WRITING:

Titles of Edited Drafts   Editing Date

WRITING STRENGTHS:

NEEDS   CONFERENCES

of these could be categorized together. During the brainstorming, all the student ideas are scripted without adding any of teachers'. Teacher ideas are added only when the students have omitted criteria we believe to be important. The students determine the weighting of the criteria or how the points will be allotted for the criteria. This is then typed and distributed to all of the students. Thus as they are working on their drafts, the criteria for evaluation are already present and available to them for reference. What follows is an example of student-generated criteria.

ASSESSMENT CRITERIA

1. Creativity and Imagination
   - details included to interest the reader
   - simile and/or metaphor included

   /6

2. Story Structure/Plot
   - beginning, middle and ending of the story are included

   /5

3. Organization
   - composition and picture sheet are complete and handed in on time

   /2

4. Sentence Fluency
   - sentences are fluent and grammatically correct

   /5

5. Conventions of Writing
   - spelling and punctuation are correct
   - story is completed in good copy form (in pen or word processed)

   /2

Comments:

TOTAL   /20

---

4. A Term Plan/Grading

Early in the term, explain how students will be evaluated for writers workshop so that they are clear about this process. The number of final drafts written for the term, the quality of those drafts, the variety of genres reflected in their writing, their ability to use class time effectively, and their development as an author are all being monitored. As a guideline, we often suggest that for an A grade they:

- have written at least five final drafts that demonstrate their ability to write a variety of genres with powerful results
- have used class and conference time effectively
- have demonstrated strong development in the writing skills highlighted in editing and in our conferences

This information is articulated for each of the letter grades to reduce the anxiety for students who are unsure of expectations. It enables all students to be more goal directed. It is also a good introduction for parents who have not experienced a writing program such as this.

5. Author's Checklist

The **Author's Checklist** highlights the six categories that will be used to evaluate student writing skills. This was adapted from Spandel and Stiggins (Spandel, Vicki and Richard J. Stiggins, *Creating Writers: Linking Assessment and Writing Instruction*. New York: Longman, 1990). These categories are discussed at length in subsequent mini-lessons throughout the year, driven by the needs of the students.

6. End of Term — Handing In and Self-Evaluation

At the end of the term on the appointed day, all the authors hand in the term's work, including all of the drafts they have written. A sheet, completed by the author, outlines all of the compositions that are completed to final draft form. The drafts are arranged with all of the working drafts paper-clipped behind the final draft to demonstrate the progression of drafts and the influence of time and editing that led to the finished copy. For the first two terms, the students select two finished drafts from the term's work that they feel are the ones that best represent their skills as an author. They complete a self-evaluation for each of these compositions using the categories from the Author's Checklist. Self-evaluation is a very important aspect of the writers workshop program. Reflection

Author's Checklist — Adapted from Spandel and Stiggins

IDEAS AND CONTENT
( ) Writing has a clear purpose.
( ) Main idea is included, with relevant details.
( ) Irrelevant details are left out.
( ) Writing shows thoughtfulness — I know what I am talking about.

ORGANIZATION
( ) Good lead.
( ) Organization makes sense and is easy to follow.
( ) Details support a big idea or a conclusion.
( ) The ending works — it is not too sudden or too late.

VOICE
( ) The writing really shows how I think and feel.
( ) I am satisfied with what I have written.
( ) The writing has my personal stamp on it.
( ) I have thought about how a reader will think and feel when reading my writing.

WORD CHOICE
( ) My words paint a picture in your mind when reading.
( ) I have used my own words in new and different ways.
( ) My writing sounds natural.
( ) My writing makes you feel as if you are there with me.

SENTENCE FLUENCY
( ) My sentences make sense.
( ) My sentences are varied in length and in word order.
( ) I have reread my paper. It flows smoothly.

CONVENTIONS
( ) I have proofread for spelling.
( ) I have read my paper aloud to myself to proofread for grammar.
( ) I have proofread for punctuation and capitalization.
( ) I have used paragraphs appropriately.
( ) My use of skills makes my paper reader friendly.

on one's work teaches the students to ask themselves questions about their writing and reinforces the skills used by good authors. It enables students to be the first judge of work that they have produced, while it allows an outside reader to notice which aspects of the writing are of greatest pride and import to the student.

7. Writer's Contract

At the beginning of the second term, each student signs a **Writer's Contract** outlining the number of completed compositions she or he will write during the term. This contract is specifically delayed until the second term since many of the students have no idea about the amount of writing they can complete within a term until they have had this experience. The contract is signed by the student, parent(s), and finally by the teacher to reinforce that we all are in agreement and support the student's goal. This number is recorded on the Term 2 sheet of editing notes so that throughout the term it can be referred to and each student is supported to remain on track for achieving his or her goal. Students keep their signed contracts in their writing folders so that they can review their writing objectives.

WRITER'S CONTRACT

Contract between _____, my parent(s)_____
/guardian

and my teacher, Ms. Feniak.

Dated on the _____ day of _____, 199 .

I have decided that from this date until the end of the term, I will complete ___ final drafts for Writers Workshop. I also agree to hand in one working draft of each of these pieces to Ms. Feniak for editing before the final draft is completed.

I am aware of the requirements (number of final drafts, variety of writing styles, quality of writing and use of class time) that are expected to achieve the grade that I am working towards for this part of my Language Arts grade.

Signed:

_____	_____	_____
student	parent(s)/guardian	teacher

WRITER'S WORKSHOP EVALUATION

Reread your Writers Workshop compositions for the term. Choose the piece that you feel demonstrates your strongest writing and evaluate it following the guidelines below.

During the term I completed _____ compositions in final draft form.

NAME: _____

A. **Ideas and Content** — Is the piece interesting, focused, detailed, and written from my experience?

Student evaluation   /5   *Teacher evaluation*   /5   /5

B. **Organization** — Does the piece have a clear introduction and ending? Changes in topic are written in a way that is not confusing to the reader. The reader's interest should be maintained throughout the composition.

Student evaluation   /5   *Teacher evaluation*   /5   /5

C. **Voice** — My composition is written using language that is natural and expresses my individuality as a writer.

Student evaluation   /5   *Teacher evaluation*   /5   /5

D. **Word Choice** — In choosing words I used verbs other than *is* and *are*, and I used clear nouns and adjectives that helped the reader understand the composition. Slang was rarely used. I used simile, metaphor, or alliteration to create strong images for the reader.

Criteria	1	2	3	4	5
Word Choice varied use of verbs, adverbs, nouns, adjectives, similes, metaphors & alliteration	repetition of words was evident which was distracting for the reader. There was a lack of descriptive vocabulary used.		able to use descriptive vocabulary to create images for the reader. A clearer picture developed as a result.		a variety of adjectives were used to create vivid or detailed images. Simile, Metaphor, and alliteration focus the reader's attention.

Student evaluation   /5   *Teacher evaluation*   /5   /5

E. **Sentence Fluency** — I combined my sentences so that they were not short and choppy. My sentences are not all the same in length and style. I am sure that my sentences are not run-on sentences. My composition could be easily read aloud without it sounding awkward.

Criteria	1	2	3	4	5
Sentence Fluency sentences are clear & easily read	sentences are short & choppy with several run-on sentences. As a result the meaning is sometimes unclear.		sentences were combined to add variety in style. Run-on sentences do not distract the reader.		there is variety in sentence length & complexity. No run-on sentences are evident. Sentences fluency is noted when read aloud.

Student evaluation /5   *Teacher evaluation* /5   /5

F. **Conventions** — Spelling, punctuation, grammar, paragraphing and other errors are not present in my final draft.

Criteria	1	2	3	4	5
Conventions spelling, punctuation, grammar & paragraphing are correct	several errors are present which distract the reader		several errors are present but they do not distract the reader.		errors, if present, are extremely minor and do not distract the reader at all

Student evaluation /5   *Teacher evaluation* /5   /5

COMMENTS:

STUDENT TOTAL /30   TEACHER TOTAL /30   /30

At the end of the term, both students and parents can determine whether or not the writing goal has been achieved. For some students, writing more compositions than stated in the contract becomes the goal, but for the majority of students, the goal set out in the contract is the one they endeavor to meet. This is a simple but quite powerful motivating factor and one that parents can be active in supporting.

8. The Final Portfolio

The last term of study is spent in compiling each student's portfolio of writing from the entire school year. The portfolio is a collection of the student's writing that shows the audience how he or she has developed as an author over the school year. The portfolio contains writing that has been selected from all the compositions. Six categories are requested, as follows:

- a satisfying piece
- an important piece
- a dissatisfying piece
- a free pick — the choice of the student
- a negotiated free pick — the choice of the student but discussed during the selection process with the teacher. The student is asked why she/he wants to include this piece.
- a second-chance piece — a composition that would benefit from a rewriting if the student had more time.

(LeMahieu, Paul. "Portfolio Assessment," paper presented at *Assessing for Success*, Richmond B.C., 1996).

These categories make the portfolios more than just a collection of student work. The portfolio should continue the learning — it is an opportunity for the student to interact with and make judgments about his or her work.

In the selection process to find a composition that matches each of these categories, the students needs to ask themselves a series of questions:

- Why did I choose this piece?
- What does it tell my audience about me as an author?
- What are the strengths and weaknesses of the piece?
- What could I do to make this a stronger piece?

Students learn this kind of questioning as the teacher models it. Post-it notes are used to mark their selections for the six categories. Since the students invariably change their minds about the compositions that best fit each category, the post-it notes are easily removed and attached to another piece as required. For many of the students, this process is one that requires some support from peers, parents, or teachers. As teachers, it is important to not choose for the student but rather to ask questions that strengthen the student's ability to reflect upon her or his writing.

Finally, when the selections are in place, a self-evaluation sheet is provided so that the students can record their reasons for the selections they chose. These reflections make it easy to evaluate how each student has developed over the year as an author. For the most part, their reasons for selecting the six compositions indicate their thoughtfulness about themselves as authors. Perhaps the most telling are their comments about the most dissatisfying piece and the second-chance piece, since these are generally not the compositions that allow the authors to feel proud. Much is learned about students through portfolio evaluation. It is a learning and evaluation tool that is accessible to all students and appropriate for all. Individual programming within a group plan thus becomes a foundation for classroom experiences for the students.

Two different student samples are included. Lewis is a skilled communicator who strives for deep expression. Janine is less developed as a writer and reader. She has had considerable support throughout the year. Notice how Janine, with support, has also achieved the expectations. Both Janine and Lewis are thoughtful and skilful in their reflections on themselves as developing writers.

Resource Role

Writers workshop can occur with or without direct resource support. Whenever the schedule permits, however, the support of a resource teacher with a strong background in language acquisition, reading, and writing is truly an asset. Typically, the resource role is that of another editor. The resource teacher picks up a student's Observations Sheet and conferences with the student. This provides more opportunity for interactive editing. Resource teachers can also adapt the mini-lesson or teach specific skills as required by the particular student with whom she is working. From time to time, some of our targeted students require

Writer's Workshop Portfolio

Author: Lewis
Number of Completed Drafts during Term Three 4.5 - 5   1997

Your portfolio of writing for the 1996-1997 school year must include 6 different pieces chosen by you which represent the following top.
- a satisfying piece
- an important piece
- a dissatisfying piece
- a free pick
- a negotiated free pick
- a second-chance piece

1. I selected __Night__ as a satisfying piece because Everything sounded right and it was easy to put together.

2. My important piece is __Thoughts__ and I believe that in this composition my writing shows development in Being able to explain what really happens when were thinking.

3. I found __Half Dead__ to be a dissatisfying piece. There are some strengths in this composition which I would like to point out, such as There aren't any strengths that I can find in this piece.

In my opinion this was not a satisfying piece however, for these reasons : Because It took me a long time to think of the lines and they still weren't good.

4. I have included __Staring Through a window__ as my free pick because I think that It was put together well and it was easy to write. It also tells a bit about how the sub-contious mind works.

5. I chose to include ___Trust___ as my negotiated free pick since it shows that as an author I can write about things that happen in the real world and it's one of my best pieces.

6. The piece which I would rework if I had time is ___Step___
I chose this composition as my second·chance piece because I think I could have used more expressive language and make it longer.

This piece could be rewritten to strengthen my writing skills in these areas My language and length.

I would leave some parts of the composition the same because I think it has some good ideas.

7. Other comments that you would like to make about your portfolio selections I don't have any other comments.

THOUGHTS   LEWIS

THOUGHTS CARRY ANSWERS
ANSWERS TO LIFE. AND ANSWERS TO QUESTIONS.
ANSWERS THAT ARE HIDDEN DEEPLY. LIKE THE TREASURES OF THE SEA.
ANSWERS THAT ARE HIDDEN VERY SHALLOWLY. LIKE COCONUTS ON A COCONUT TREE.
THINK DEEPLY. THINK BRIGHTLY.
THE ANSWERS WILL COME.
THOUGHTS CARRY ANSWERS.

important

Trust   by Lewis

An unbroken link between two beings.
Keeping truth, like an anchor holds a boat.
Destroying lies, like an exterminator does to the undesirable.
But now the bond is growing rusty and weak like an aged chain.
The bond has snapped and truth is lost.
A broken bond between two beings.

neg. free pick

Writers Workshop Portfolio

Author: Janine _____ _____ contract = 5.
Number of Completed Drafts during Term Three: 4.5 ____

Your portfolio of writing for the 1996-1997 school year must include 6 different
pieces chosen by you which represent the following topics:
- a satisfying piece
- an important piece
- a dissatisfying piece
- a free pick
- a negotiated free pick
- a second-chance piece

1. I selected __The drem__ as a satisfying piece because
I can nuever get the ending right
and I though in this story the ending was
really good.
2. My important piece is ____WAR____ and I
believe that in this composition my writing shows development in wrighting
about the .subject of war is hard
because war is killing and all about fighting.

3. I found __Mr. Shmoo__ to be a dissatisfying piece.
There are some strengths in this composition which I would like to point out,
such as I made a book for the story and It
looks really good from the out side.

In my opinion this was not a satisfying piece however, for these reasons :

4. I have included __Daddy__ as my free pick
because I think that It was a really well rote
and It also had a good ending
like the dream.

5. I chose to include _____Snow_____ as my negotiated free pick since it shows that as an author I can ryme pretty well and I like that It is like a kid poem.

6. The piece which I would rework if I had time is _____Rats_____
I chose this composition as my "second-chance" piece because it could have been alot better if I had worked hardder.

This piece could be rewritten to strengthen my writing skills in these areas to be longer and better ritten.

I would leave some parts of the composition the same because some of the story is pretty good.

7. Other comments that you would like to make about your portfolio selections well it is not about my selections but my other really important peice is shooting star.

WAR

When I run through the mud I think of stars shooting through the sky with their long beautiful tails drifting behind them, but the tail of the star frome is my gun shooting, the only thing is that a star dosent kill anyone

As I see the star playing in the sky his family and friends arood him I love to be there to

By: Janine

Writers Workshop Portfolio

Author: _____

Number of Completed Drafts during Term Three: _____

Your portfolio of writing for the school year must include 6 different pieces chosen by you which represent the following topics:
- a satisfying piece
- an important piece
- a dissatisfying piece
- a free pick
- a negotiated free pick
- a second chance piece

1. I selected _____ as a satisfying piece because

2. My important piece is _____ and I believe that in this composition my writing shows development in

3. I found _____ to be a dissatisfying piece. There are some strengths in this composition which I would like to point out, such as

   In my opinion this was not a satisfying piece however, for these reasons:

4. I have included _____ as my free pick because I think that

5. I chose to include _____ as my negotiated free pick since it shows that as an author I

6. The piece which I would rework if I had time is _____. I chose this composition as my second chance piece because

   This piece could be rewritten to strengthen my writing skills in these areas

   I would leave some parts of the composition the same because

7. Other comments that you would like to make about your portfolio selections

help getting started with writing. Although this decreases as the year continues, it is another possibility for resource support. The other, final area of support is in organization. The resource teacher frequently meets with those students for whom organization is a challenge, and helps them pull themselves together. As a team, we try to intervene and keep on-task those students who need more direct intervention. The collaborative efforts of a teacher and a resource teacher together in writers workshop decrease the marking load of the classroom teacher and provide more one-on-one or small-group focus for students within the class. Identified students are receiving support necessary for their achievement of class goals or grade expectations, rather than a separate program. They have the ongoing opportunity to learn from more powerful models of writing as provided by the class sharing, and they have the chance to become powerful models themselves within the different genres of writing that are explored. Additional planning time between the classroom teacher and the resource teacher is minimized. The impact on student learning is maximized.

4 Standard Reading Assessment

Why Are We Planning This Way?

One of the challenges in teaching is to readily determine "where the students are at" and if, indeed, this performance is reasonable. Next, of course, is to determine where along a continuum of development the class should next move, and what kind of support students need to progress. Finally, information is needed in reporting progress to parents. As teachers, we found that having a framework to help guide our instructional decisions was a bonus. We also found that regular, independent reading assessments provided immediate feedback to students and provided information to guide our instructional decisions.

Helping Students Assess Their Developing Skills

The **Standard Reading Assessment** became one of the pieces in our assessment file. The assessments occurred regularly, without prior teaching, and were used to keep the students informed of their performance and their progress measured against a bigger picture, or framework for reading, using the first four (of six) levels described in the K-12 Reading Reference Set (B.C. Ministry of Education and Ministry Responsible for Multiculturalism and Human Rights, Evaluating Reading Across the Curriculum: *Using the Reading Reference Set to Support Learning and Enhance Communication*. Victoria, BC: 1994.) Our primary goal was to monitor students' independent application of the skills and strategies we were teaching in our reading program. A second goal was to help students become aware of personally appropriate reading goals. Thus, they were also becoming familiar with what they needed to do next to become more sophisticated, effective readers. The framework was based on the premise that readers make meaning by interacting with text. Acknowledging that different readers make different meanings based on their prior knowledge, their skills, the chosen material, their engagement as readers, "all effective readers are able to demonstrate the relationship between their interpretations and the written text" (p. 3). A reading experience includes both a context (the text and the amount of support provided) and the reading (strategies/approaches, accuracy/comprehension, and response).

For the purpose of the Standard Reading Assessment, we decided to control the context by using a common text and initially providing no support. The individual reading could then be judged in terms of strategies/approaches, accuracy/comprehension, and response. We recognize that reading is complex and one snapshot assessment does not provide a complete picture. We try to repeat these assessments every four to six weeks and to use the information from them to guide our teaching. We also use the framework to build criteria with students and to guide other classroom assessments in different contexts.

Initially, the texts we chose came from *Reading and Responding — Evaluation Resources for Your Classroom* (Jeroski, Sharon, Faye Brownlie and Linda Kaser [grades 4, 5 and 6]. Scarborough, ON: Nelson Canada, 1990, 1991). These books provided poems, information articles, and narrative text to use for assessment at each grade level. Having a ready supply of good materials is an asset. As we continue with the assessments, however, we find ourselves writing some of the material and choosing other material from classroom texts, brochures and magazines, and newspapers. We also write our own response questions or reuse response questions such as "Using your ideas, feelings and images, show me you understand..." or "What two questions would you like to ask the author?" or "How does the information you have read connect with what you believed to be true before reading? Is this new information convincing enough for you to change your ideas? Why or why not?"

The classroom teacher and resource teacher work side by side in this assessment. With practice, an assessment can be completed in forty-five minutes.

The Assessment Process

1. A passage and its response sheet are chosen and distributed to each student.
2. The teacher reads the title of the passage, and then invites the students to read the passage, circling words with which they are unfamiliar. Students are also encouraged to preview the response sheet before reading, as this will help set a purpose for reading.
3. As the students are reading and responding, the teacher moves from student to student and listens to them read. The student chooses a piece of the text which he or she has already practised. The teacher takes the student's piece of text (which may have circled words on it), gives the student her clean copy, and records how well the student reads. She notices:

omissions	repetitions
substitutions	insertions
reversals	don't know (when the word given to the student)
self-corrections	

Prior to leaving the student, the teacher writes a quick compliment about the reading on the student's page.
4. Once all students have had an opportunity to give an oral reading sample and have completed their responses, all of the papers are collected for scoring. (These include both the student copy of the text and the student response sheet.)
5. All students are included in this assessment. Adaptations are made as necessary for Level 1 ESL and students with severe reading difficulties.

6. *Scoring*: The text and date of the assessment are recorded. Any information that has been observed from the oral reading sample, interaction with the student, and the student's response sheet is recorded. We choose a different color of highlight pen for each assessment. Over time, a pattern emerges. By reporting period or the end of the year, this sheet has a great deal of information on it about the student's reading performance in independent, text-imposed situations. The information can be read at a glance. The evidence to support these interpretations is stapled to the crib sheet. An example follows. The dated words are those that the student miscued on each passage.

Using the Information

Assessments are worth doing when they give teachers information to inform their practice. The following scenarios are typical of the action taken as a result of information collected on the class assessment.

1. Building Criteria for Powerful Response

From time to time, the teacher chooses five or six student response samples (preferably a variety of representations — web, paragraph, pictures…), makes them into overhead transparencies, and shares them with the class. Samples are chosen because they are powerful in some way; they have achieved some of the descriptions of more sophisticated reading behaviour. The samples are shown to the class, one at a time, with the comment "I have chosen a variety of your responses to use as samples. These samples will help us build criteria for what really works or what is powerful in this type of response." The question posed to the students is "What strikes you as powerful about this sample?" or "What do you notice that really works in this sample?" The questions are positive and only positive comments are accepted. These comments are recorded on the chalkboard or on chart paper.

Once all the response samples have been reviewed, the teacher and the class review their comments and reorganize them into a more coherent form. These then are posted and guide other text responses the students might be doing over the next four to six weeks — that is, allowing them to practise the desired behaviours in a variety of supported and

Standard Reading Assessment

Context	Date	Strategies	Accuracy	Response
		· recognizes some words · uses illustrations · uses some text cues	· recognizes topic	· connects reading with own experience · evaluates story
		↓	↓	↓
		· gist not word/word · self-corrects · asks for help · pictures and text cues · phonics · miscues make sense	· gist and main events · subtleties/details when questioned	· connects to stories, information, experience · responds personally, retells, evaluates
		↓	↓	↓
		· comfortable · aware of how he/she is reading · predicts, previews · monitors for sense · uses context cues	· explicit ideas and details · needs support with implicit information or relationship	· reflects on reading · responds with ideas, images and feelings · works alone or together to respond beyond immediate reaction
		↓	↓	↓
		· adapts for purpose · focuses for longer times · returns to same task/material over time	· recall and relationships · support inferences with specific text references · research includes several texts	· responds with explicit connections to knowledge and experiences · beyond simple judgments

Reading Reference Set, B.C. Ministry of Education, 1993   adapted by Faye Brownlie, 1997

Standard Reading Assessment

Name: _____

Class: _____

Context	Date	Strategies	Accuracy	Response
				· provides support: reasons and explanations · responds over time · connects to social concerns and issues beyond classroom
		· confident · sense of knowing how to... · understands readers' role · understands meaning is readers' knowing, feeling, doing and what writer does	· literal and inferential · fills in gaps in text, connects ideas from different parts of text · recognize relationships · uses details and subtleties to make generalizations	· extends material in response and interpretation · connects to personal information and universal themes, global issues · explains criteria when judging · reads critically
		↓	↓	↓
		· independent · uses previous knowledge and approaches · creates context for decon-textualized material	· explicit and implicit information and ideas in abstract, complex text · can use ambiguous language, structure, ideas for relevant conclusions and interpretations · different interpretations	· new insights · literary — symbolic and literary features · informative — divergent point of view, multiple possibilities, connections · sustained exploration and reflection

unsupported contexts before being assessed again. This criterion list is also used for students to self-assess their responses from the assessment and to then set a personal reading goal for the next month. These goals will vary greatly from student to student, but each student is choosing a goal within the context of the class goals and graded curriculum expectations. Patterns noticed in the class's reading behavior indicate direction for teaching in the next four to six weeks.

These grade 6 and 7 students have responded to an information text "Pollution Blamed for Seal Deaths" (*Reading and Responding*, grade 6). They had been asked: "Using any form you choose, show me you understand the selection you have read. Remember to use your ideas, images and feelings from your reading."

In the criteria building session, Ronnie's is the first sample. The students notice that Ronnie has shown *cause and effect* (the factories and the toxic wastes in the water, and *emotion* (the seal cub calling out to the mother).

Michelle's is the second sample and the students add *main idea and some good details from the article* and *summary* to the list.

Pollution Blamed For Seal Deaths

Because of pollution, about 7 000 harbour seals have died. In West Germans waters, another 2 000 have died. This has been one of the worster ecology d.s.r. Each year, 400 000 tonnes of oil leak into the ocean. Too much ~~Pollution~~ toxic waste are dumped in the ocean. Scientist have found tumors and lesions in fish, caused by the toxic waste.

Finally, Anita's sample is shown. The students notice her *details from the text* and the *relationships* shown on her web.

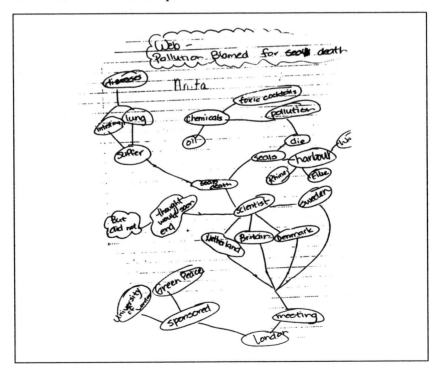

The criteria list that is posted includes:

- main idea and some specific details
- emotional connection
- how ideas fit together — their relationship to each other
- extending — thinking beyond the text
- cause and effect
- summary — be sure we can tell you have read the text, not just used your own ideas

2. Small Group Support

If a small group of students experience great difficulty with reading the text or with a particular response, these students redo the challenging part of the assessment, with support. Later in the week, either the classroom teacher or the resource teacher collects the students, the text that they read, and their responses. Together, they first look at the words the students have circled and discuss how to say these words and possible meanings. Next, they choose a part of the text to read aloud together, discussing as they read the connections they are making and what they are thinking about. Finally, they return to the response. If the students have been asked to respond to more than one question, only one is chosen to redo.

Together, the question is read and ways to respond to the question are discussed. When the teacher is confident that this entire group of students is more able to respond to the question, they redo the one question. These responses are marked "with support," rescored, and charted on the crib sheet with the symbol WS, to indicate what the student could do with support. This not only allows the students direct instruction for desired achievement but also boosts their confidence, because they have now witnessed themselves as more able to perform. From the teacher's perspective, she has specific information on where the students were experiencing difficulty, and on what strategies were effective in supporting the student. These, then, are applied, as appropriate, in a variety of contexts in the next four to six weeks.

Notice the change in Christine's response to this prompt from a grade 5 selection "Flying" (*Reading and Responding*, grade 5), "Using your ideas, feelings, and images, show me in writing that you understand the story."

My Ideas are: That he didn't really
know what a flying machine really
was so he asked Someone.

(c support)

Christine _____ December 11, 1997

(Thought)

He was thinking about his, flying
machine because other people were
laughing at him. He thought that he was
the first person to invent a flying machine.
the other people were thinking an
airplane was a flying machine.

3. Vocabulary

As we are scoring the responses, miscued words are noted. Individual lists are dated and charted on the student's sheet. This is particularly helpful with students who are learning English. Initially these students often have a long list of words. They become very proud of their accomplishments as they see the list diminish as they acquire English vocabulary. These words can be read and talked about in small groups, with the resource teacher. Sometimes the students practise these new "hard" words for homework.

A class list of miscued words is also kept. In mini-lessons of five to ten minutes over the next two weeks, the teacher returns to these words and studies them with the class. This study includes strategies for decoding the words such as phonics and structural analysis, and strategies for making sense of the meaning.

4. Preparation for the Next Standard Reading Assessment

At the beginning of the next assessment, the students revisit the criteria developed from the five or six student response samples. This assessment may be a different reading, genre or the response questions may be quite different. Together, the students and teacher review the criteria and decide on which of those items listed will be important to consider in this assessment. They may add or delete items. The students are also reminded of their reading goal. They are invited to think about the criteria prior to reading, "When you begin to demonstrate your understanding, what will you keep I mind?" Following the assessment, they return to their response and reflect, "What should I notice that you did today?" (referenced to the criteria) and "What will I keep in mind for next month?"

5 Literature Circles

Key Ingredients to Reading Comprehension

Linda Fielding and David Pearson synthesized thirty years of research in the field of reading comprehension and found four key ingredients to successful reading comprehension programming:

1. large amounts of time for actual text reading
2. teacher-directed instruction in comprehension strategies
3. opportunities for peer and collaborative learning
4. occasions for students to talk to a teacher and one another about their responses to reading. (Fielding, Linda and David Pearson, "Reading Comprehension: What Works," in *Educational Leadership*, Volume 51, #5, Feb. 94.)

As resource teachers, one of our responsibilities is to share current research with teachers and to help them implement the implications of this research. Our conversation began as we applied these key ingredients to the class's current reading program. We decided that with the current common practice of one or two group novels students were engaged in many authentic strategies, taught through direct instruction and modeling, then encouraged to use these strategies and the thinking behind them in their personal reading. Students often worked collaboratively to problem solve, connect their experiences with the reading, or to extend and personalize their thinking as a result of reading. In these instances, they were frequently called upon to reflect on the processes they were using, to share and record their reflections, and to set goals for further refinement of their personal use of strategies and collaborative skills for the next time. Thus, in reflection, we felt that current strengths in our reading programming included #2, teacher-directed instruction in comprehension strategies and #3, opportunities for peer and collaborative learning.

The downside, however, was twofold. We had previously queried whether or not students were actually involved enough in reading on their own. Did they have sufficient time for #1, large amounts of time for actual text reading? Furthermore, when we did plan for USSR (Uninterrupted Sustained Silent Reading) it was common practice to read for fifteen or twenty minutes, and then turn to another subject, with no time for reflection, sharing, talk, or another response to the books they had been reading. The response part of our reading program could certainly use development.

Many of the students did not read widely on their own. Class composition included a significant number of less-developed readers, two virtual nonreaders, several voracious readers, a low-incidence student with Down syndrome, and several ESL students, none of whom were in their first year of learning English. We wanted them to read and read, to come to love reading, to read thoughtfully, and to want to continue to read independently. With this in mind we turned to our version of Literature Circles.

The Plan — Creating Readers

We first visited our local children's bookstore and asked them for a group of novels that would grab our class of grade 4 and 5 students and we began reading. From this event, the following novels were chosen:

The Ghost of Popcorn Hill — Betty Ren Wright
The Castle in the Attic — Elizabeth Winthrop
Mixed-Up Stories from Wayside School — Louis Sachar
Jacob's Little Giant — Barbara Smucker
Why Are the Best Clues Always Found in the Garbage? — Linda Bailey
Stone Fox — John Reynolds Gardiner

Six copies of each book were purchased. The books ranged in difficulty, style, and interest. They had both male and female protagonists, urban and rural settings, current and historical time periods. Several of the books were part of a series, so students could become turned on to authors.

For the first three days, we worked together in the class. We also worked in ninety-minute segments, which for most classes is a large chunk of time. This was a major portion of the resource time allotted for this class. After the first week, resource support during literature circles occurred for one of these ninety-minute periods per week. The schedule for the first three days follows:

Day One

Introduce the students to **Book Conversations.** Introduce the books to the students. Students choose their first book and begin reading.

Day Two

Meet with a group of students who are reading the same book while students in other books continue reading. Students are to come to the meeting with a brief passage prepared to read aloud. This becomes the start of the discussion as other students say something about what they think when they hear this section or when they read it themselves. Teachers try to mediate the conversation but not lead it. The goal is for the students to have this conversation without a teacher present. Plan for fifteen minutes conversation with each group.

Day Three

Ensure that all groups have had an opportunity to meet in their first literature circle. Allow lots of time for individual reading. Use this time to meet with less-developed readers individually and monitor their reading progress using the framework. Near the end of the class, ask the students to begin their **Response Logs**.

By the end of the third day, with both teachers present, less-developed readers will have all had an individual conference, all students will have met in a literature circle, and all students will have written one response.

In the following weeks, twice a week, students respond in writing in their response logs to connect their reading to their experiences to their knowledge.

Every two weeks, a new comprehension strategy is introduced. The strategy is modeled with the class, and then students work with the strategy using their current novel.

The Event — "Grand Conversations"

Excitement ran rampant when the students discovered that we had a new box of books for them. We wanted our students to engage in "grand conversations," conversations where they came to new understandings (Wells, Gordon. *The Meaning Makers. Children Learning Language and Using Language to Learn*. Portsmouth, NH: Heinemann, 1986). We thought, since this was a new practice to us, this might be challenging to our students. We also were familiar with Lee McGee's research suggesting that there were three kinds of talk in these grand conversations:

1. "mucking about," where the talk rambles and is only loosely tied together (Short, Kathy. "Creating a Community of Learners," in *Talking About Books: Creating Literate Communities*, Kathy Short and Kathryn Pierce, Ed. Portsmouth, NH: Heinemann, 1990.)
2. weaving through or saying for others, where ideas are restated
3. focusing on a sustained inquiry about an issue where talk helps us say the new and utterances and turns are closely tied together (McGee, Lee. "Grand Conversations as Social Contexts for Literary Work". Paper presented at the American Education Research Association Conference, April 1996, New York City).

We wanted them to be successful right from the beginning, so we began by practising how to talk about a piece of text.

We placed a poem on the overhead, read it aloud two times, and asked the students to say something about what they were thinking about the poem. As they spoke, we gently wove in and out of their responses, giving our "notice that's" about what they were saying. These comments of ours were drawn from both McGee's frame and our desire to help them link their experiences and knowledge in new ways with the poem. We practised these conversations with two poems and explained to the students that this would be the crux of the following weeks of reading. They would be asked to say something in a variety of contexts — in small-group conversations, in response journals, perhaps in private conversations. We would be helping them to become more sophisticated in their ability to talk about texts.

All of the books were introduced to the class prior to their making a personal choice. A pattern emerged as to how they were introduced.

- Read a page.
- Describe the kind of reader who might enjoy this book — male/female hero, setting, challenge, readers who like camping, computers, mystery, historical fiction...
- Describe the length of the book, type size, and pictures... "If you are very busy just now with soccer, you might find that reading this book will take too long."

All books were introduced with equal status. Nothing was referred to as easier!

Students were asked to choose two books, in case their first choice was gone. As they chose their books, we respected all choices, and they began reading.

As the second day began, several students entered the class announcing that they had finished their book! This caused a considerable flurry in the class as they headed off for a second choice. We established a book chart. Students' names were listed down the side of the chart. As they chose a new book, they entered the name of the book by their name. This enabled us to both keep track of their reading and to call students together to meet in their literature circles based on texts they might already have read.

The conversations in the literature circles ran quite smoothly. As teachers, we were challenged to listen to the students and to resist the urge to question them in a traditional manner. Students were able to talk about their books and their reactions to them, without telling the events of the story before others had read as far. We tried to meet with students in groups once or twice a week.

After students had written two different responses in their response journals, we noticed a pattern emerging in their writing. Either they retold what they had read or they began "This reminds me of a time when,..." and we were unable to determine any connections to the text. We decided to develop criteria with the students for powerful responses.

We asked for three volunteers who would be willing to put their writing up for analysis. To do this, each student would choose one of his responses and read it aloud to the class. The class audience would listen for what struck them about the response. From the student samples read, the following list of criteria was established:

- recommendation: Who? Why?
- summary, very brief
- genre: What kind of book? Is this a good example?
- opinions: supported with details and evidence from the book
- connections: book to own life and experiences
- Does this book relate to others you have read? How?
- type of vocabulary used

These criteria were posted. As students continued their responses, they were referred to. Often students were asked to respond to specific criteria on the list. Often they were asked to reflect on their response and to notice which of the criteria they had met in their response. The responses became much more powerful as a result of this process and its continued use. Notice Jon's response after working with the criteria for several weeks.

Jacob's Little Giant

This book is an excellent book. It is about a boy named Jacob. Nothing seems to go right for him. One day a man comes by with two Giant Canada geese. It is Jacob's job to take care of them. He gets the Giant Canada Geese all settled in and they make a nest and lay some eggs. They hatch. There are five gosling. Jacob is so happy. He feeds the goslings every day and they become very healthy. Then all of a sudden, the fox comes and kills one of the goslings. Some hunters come and shoot Little Giant in the wing. Little Giant is the smallest gosling. He is also Jacob's favorite gosling. He gets all fixed up and the little goose gets to go back to his family. One day Jacob and his friend Amos are fishing for a "mile long pike" that lives in their pond. Jacob catches him but he lets go. There is another fox and he is trying to get the geese. Jacob chased him away. The pike got away but Jacob saved his goslings.

I recommend this book for all ages. This book is a book most people would like. Most people would like this book because it is a fast moving book. The characters are very interesting. I found Jacob interesting because he cared about other people, even geese. He is very slow to anger. He didn't even get mad when Amos said, "That was a dumb thing to do to let go of the rod." He is a tender person. His feeling can be hurt easily. I think the author of this book put a lot of effort into this book. This book has powerful words in and the author used her imagination. I think everyone should read this book.

New comprehension strategies were introduced about every second week. Since the students were writing regularly in their response journals, we attempted to choose strategies that would address different representations or different intelligences. We would teach a strategy to the class, and then have them apply this to whichever book they were currently reading. Strategies included:

Venn Diagrams

Compare two characters in your novel or two settings or problems from two novels that you have read.

Tableaus

A team of students who have read the same book meet and decide on a specific scene in the book that they could portray. They form the scene with their bodies and freeze in position. A student from the audience taps each member of the scene, who then explains who he is and his importance or relevance at this time.

Hot Seat or Talk Shows

A team of students who have read the same book meet and assign characters. One of them becomes the interviewer (or the person holding the mike), and the audience (the class) questions the panel. Members of the panel answer in role.

Composing a Rap

Alone or with a partner, compose and perform a rap that tells a part of your story and your thinking about it.

Learning Journeys

Students were given the following legend. They were asked to consider a goal that a character in their novel had and the path that she or he took to achieve this goal. This would be their learning journey. They would then map the journey of their character, using the icons from the legend. (See page 70.)

Containers for Characters

Each student was given Plasticene™ and asked to design a container to represent him/herself and to decorate it with three symbols showing what was important to him/her. A second piece of Plasticene was used to build a container for a character in the novel and to decorate this with three symbols showing what was important to the character.

Evaluation

1) With the resource teacher, students at risk and other targeted students had a reading conference once a week, following a format similar to that of the literature circle. This provided a time for direct teaching of specific skills, an opportunity to practise to enhance performance in the literature circle, and an opportunity to monitor the individual student's progress.

2) Students were asked to submit three response samples from their response journals that best indicated their response performance. The collection of responses needed to meet all the criteria, not each individual response. These were graded against a four- point scale, built from their criteria.

---

4 All criteria met.
3 One of the criteria is missing or not well developed.
2 Several of the criteria are missing. Thoughtful interaction with the
   text is not evident.
1 The task or the text is inappropriate for the student at this time.

---

3) Comprehension products were to demonstrate:
   - explicit ideas and details from the novel
   - relationships of ideas and details from the novel
   - inferences supported with specific text reference

These criteria were adapted from the framework, so assessment goals and instruction were strongly linked.

Resource Role

The resource teacher had initiated this unit of study. We believe this is one of the tasks of the resource teacher — to bring research and fresh ideas to the classroom. The plan for implementing literature circles had been co-developed by the teacher and the resource teacher. During the implementation time, the resource teacher continued to monitor the targeted students, but also worked with other members of the class. We teachers found it easy to communicate with one another about the goals of the targeted students and about how we were adapting the class curricular expectations and the support necessary to achieve these.

6 Poetry: Three Invitations

1. Discussion Groups

Changing Our Approach to Poetry

Too often, poetry has been omitted in grades four to seven or has been taught in a very traditional style that relied on the teacher's imparting her interpretation of a poem. This "match my thinking" approach to poetry tends to be exclusive. If we change our approach to the teaching of poetry, we become less apprehensive about this genre, and we include more students.

Each reader brings a unique blend of experiences and background knowledge to reading. These become the lenses for making sense of or interpreting a poem. In discussion groups, students can share their interpretations, refine their ideas, discover new ways of looking at a poem, and determine which interpretation works best for them. This networking of thinking is both expansive and supportive. It encourages students to read and respond to poetry and to incorporate the precise language of poetry in their oral and written language.

Involving Students in Discussion

The process of involving groups of students in discussion about a poem is a simple one. The first step is to read the poem orally to the students so that they can hear the poem and the pronunciation of the language. The students then are given the opportunity to ask questions about words or phrases that are unclear to them. Each student then receives a copy of the poem and is asked to join a group of three or four students, chosen in advance by the teacher to be a heterogeneous group.

Once students are settled in their groups, they are asked to read the poem silently, jotting down notes about their ideas and questions as they read. When this is complete, the group selects a volunteer to orally read the poem once again. Students then are given several minutes to determine what they wish to say about the poem; each student will be given an opportunity to share an idea, observation, or question about the poem. This sharing is done with students following in order around the circle. When sharing of ideas is occurring, only the student who is speaking may add ideas. The others are asked not to add any comments until it is their turn. This allows individual students to share ideas without having to justify or defend their point of view. It also gives the rest of the group a chance to really listen to each person's comments, which, in turn, may clarify their own thinking about the poem. In this stage of the process, students are practising the skills needed for reflective listening. For students who are learning English, sharing their ideas in a small group is somewhat easier than in a class discussion. To provide support for these students and others who require additional support to participate, model some questions or comment starters to use when sharing their thinking. This modeling should occur prior to the groups beginning their discussion, so the less-facile language users come with advance preparation to the discussion. Either the resource teacher or the classroom teacher can provide this support. Examples of these starters are:

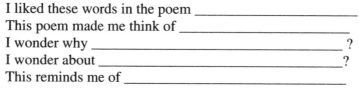

I liked these words in the poem _____

This poem made me think of _____

I wonder why _____ ?

I wonder about _____ ?

This reminds me of _____

After all group members have shared their opinions, they then discuss various aspects of the poem that were raised by the members of the group. At this point, students can speak in a discussion format. Remind the students to seek evidence or examples from the poem to back up their ideas. They then try to reach a consensus about what they feel the poem is trying to convey. Often, a four- to six-minute timeframe is sufficient to complete this portion of the activity. The time constraint tends to focus students' conversation on being on-task. Each group then chooses a spokesperson who will explain the group's interpretation of the poem to the rest of the class. These spokespeople must listen carefully to what is described by the others so that they can build upon, or concur with, the observations made by the rest of the groups.

Evaluation

Throughout this process, circulate among the groups to provide assistance to those students who are having difficulty expressing their ideas due to shyness, limited English, communication problems, or special educational needs. Other students will not be distracted when suggestions are offered quietly to students who are having difficulty. They learn to wait for the students to explain her or his idea and to support them in expressing themselves. These skills are necessary for all to develop, as there are times when every learner will need the support of a group in order to express him/herself clearly.

This is an appropriate time to jot down anecdotal observations of how well the students are working on the task. To reinforce positive ways of participating in a discussion, record authentic language used by students in the room. These anonymous responses can later be shared with the class, asking them to comment on how these phrases facilitate communication. Searching for and making explicit new and more effective ways to communicate with others is ongoing. These notes are kept to form a term report card comment on communication and working with others.

2. Three-Dimensional Poetry

Moving Beyond Language and Discussion

One of the many ways to engage students in thinking about poetry is to have them interpret a poem and present their understanding of its meaning in a three-dimensional form. This engages the verbal/linguistic intelligence, the visual/spatial intelligence, and the bodily/kinesthetic intelligence. Moving beyond language and discussion invites more students into making meaning of the poem and increases their chance of success. In choosing a way to visually show an audience what a poem is about, the students need to become familiar with what they believe the poet is trying to express. The skills they learned in the poetry discussion groups will help the students to focus on imagery within the poem, identify poetic devices that the poet has used within the poem, and determine the theme of the poem.

Describing a Theme Three-Dimensionally

This assignment tends to be highly motivational to students. They are given a choice of using one of the poems they have written or of choosing a poem from any source as long as they credit the poet. Their task is to think of a way to show the theme or meaning of the poem to someone who cannot read. Giving the students an open-ended choice such as this can be difficult. It is advisable to provide a rich and varied selection of poetry from anthologies and collections by various poets to assist the students in finding a poem that interests them. A great deal of reading of poetry happens during this search time! The students then "test" the poem by reading and rereading it to determine whether or not they can identify its theme.

Some students love the nonsense poetry of Jack Prelutsky and Shel Silverstein. Deciding on a theme with this poetry can be very challenging, however, and is not always appropriate. If students are really set on using a poem like this, ask them to show the essence of the poem's humour in their representation. This works well for many students who are not easily engaged by poetry. The requirement that they must show the humour in the poem in a three-dimensional format is every bit as challenging as showing the theme of another kind of poem.

After they have selected a poem, the students then need to decide on the type of representation they will use to show the poem to an audience. Representations include: dioramas, mobiles, clay or Plasticine™, fabric figures, wire sculptures, handmade puppets, paper and multimedia collage. The list of possibilities is almost endless. Before the students begin to construct their representations of the poems, they produce a list of materials they will require. They are given the responsibility for locating each of the items.

Evaluation

This is not a homework assignment. We value the interaction among students in the creation of their representations, the problem solving, and the sharing of poetry that envelop the class. Thus class time is provided to design and construct the representations. Again, with anecdotal comments, information is collected on the skills employed to problem solve during the design process. Individual students are also interviewed about how their representation fits the theme or message about the poem that they want to express.

Student work is judged according to how well the criteria have been met.

- a theme is identified (or humour)
- a three-dimensional representation is made of this theme
- the theme is supported with text evidence

As well, students are asked to reflect, in writing, on which aspect of this project they are most proud.

The final component of this assignment is a recitation of the poem by the student for the rest of the class. After the recitation, the student displays his/her three-dimensional representation, tells how it fits the theme of the poem, and explains which aspect of the project has made him/her the most proud.

The criteria for the oral presentation include:

- voice quality
- expression
- eye contact with audience
- students' own perception of how well their project expresses the poem in terms of its materials, format, and representation of the theme.

Both sets of criteria can be scored on a four-point scale:

4 Moves beyond all the criteria.
3 Meets all the criteria.
2 Barely meets the criteria — usually has difficulty in defending the theme.
1 Meets few of the criteria.

This information is valuable when it comes time to writing the Language Arts portion of the report card for each student. From this activity, we have collected information about comprehension of a poem, information about solving problems along the way, information about students' ability to express themselves both in the physical representation of the poem as well as orally in front of the class as an audience, and a reflection about which aspect of this made them most proud. This form of feedback helps learners become more intrinsically motivated. They are then prepared to take risks in allowing themselves to experiment with more creative ways of expressing their understanding. As teachers, we try to foster this kind of environment by changing the ways we give feedback about their learning to our students.

3. Architectural Tours*

Taking Students into the Community

All of our communities have unique architecture that is often overlooked in our daily lives. Investigating the local architectural styles helps students learn about the history of their community. Again, this is highly motivating for students as it takes them out of the classroom, helps nurture keen powers of observation, and then leads to showing their understanding in free-verse poetry.

Providing a Framework for Student Learning

Initially, the teacher must gather information about the building to be explored. In one case, we studied Aberthau, a house in Vancouver whose name means, "a place filled with light." Prior to arriving with the students, we toured the house, made quick sketches of several architectural details in the house, and identified the architects as Samuel MacLure and Cecil Fox. These names then led us to the library to locate books about their architectural style and other buildings in the area.

Next, we selected six features of the house on which to focus. In this case, they included the porte-cochère, the stained glass and mullioned windows, the mock half-timbering, the newel posts, the parquet flooring, and the fireplace in the sitting room. It is important to have planned your focus features. When guiding students through a building, each focus features becomes a point of discussion and a time of sketching. It is at these times that historical stories are wrapped around an explanation of the features to build an historical context for the students.

Consider which questions would support the students building an understanding of the features. These questions provide a framework for learning and can be discussed in small groups or partners as the students tour. For example, we asked students to consider why the porte-cochère, a covered entry porch for people entering or leaving vehicles, was incorporated as a design feature of the house. This prompted a lively discussion about the kinds of vehicles, mainly horse-drawn carriages, which were the mode of transportation at that time. The students also pointed out that the amount of rainfall in Vancouver and the resulting mud made the porte-cochere a must in terms of functional design.

Students stop with the teacher at each of the six focus points. At this time, they hear a brief overview or story about the feature, attempt to capture the feature in a sketch, consider a question or two about the feature, and collect notes on what they have seen and heard.

Once the tour is complete, students sit with a partner, show their illustrations to each other and discuss the features of the building which they found to be most interesting. Following this, they circle ideas, words, or phrases they feel are particularly descriptive. Each student is asked to contribute one. The teacher records these to make them accessible to all. Some of the phrases our students shared were:

"Looking through the old stained glass is like looking back in time"

"...shimmering, shining Mother of Pearl"

"...intricate tiled patterns"

"...a multitude of fireplaces"

"A rainforest of wood flooring"

"...damaged by weather and time"

"Stained glass windows dimmed by renovations"

Students now begin a free-verse poem about a particular aspect of the house or their overall impression of the house. To build this poem, they can use the class phrases, their own phrases, or the information contained in their sketches.

For students who require adaptation of this writing assignment, they can choose six to ten phrases from the class collection, practise reading them with the teacher or with a partner, choose an order for the phrases, and have this be their poem. This is a valid representation of their experience in the house, but is scaffolded with others' language. This borrowing from others is one of the ways that language becomes our own.

Evaluation

After several minutes of drafting their poems, students can share their leads or beginning drafts. Together they work to develop criteria. The Evaluation Sheet and poems are the work of students in this grade five to seven group.

Student Free-Verse Poems

many people
milling around
dancing and strutting
through the party
I must escape the noise
I rush up the stairs
and onto the landing.
The sun, low in the sky
shines through the patterned stained glass
shined oak and polished mahogany
greet me in my retreat.
 Lea

Designed glass
will make the light
go dancing
by the twisting patterns
on the great oak floor
the coloured light betrays
the presence of dust which
clings to the flowers
that hang over the doors.

Danielle

From the window
in my carriage
I can see
the biggest buildings
When I step in and see
such a beauty
for a moment I think
I own the whole thing.
Then I go through
the building with care.
 Cam

* Many thanks to Vancouver teacher and author Jan Wells for her help with the Alberta lesson design and to Richmont teacher Tina Pali for her help with theFree-Verse Evaluation Form.

Free-Verse Evaluation Sheet: _____

Word Choice

- each word is carefully chosen to create a strong image, sound, feeling, smell, or taste
- more than one of the 5 senses are used
- language specific to the architecture of the house is used

Student Evaluation /5   *Teacher Evaluation /5*

Voice

a *personal* impression of the house or some aspect of the house is developed

Student Evaluation /3   *Teacher Evaluation /3*

Flow

ideas connect together to create an image or an idea

Student Evaluation /3   *Teacher Evaluation /3*

Ideas and Content

you stick to your topic
you help the reader learn about the house and its specifics

Student Evaluation /4   *Teacher Evaluation /4*

Givens (your verse will be returned and you will lose 1 mark for missing each of the following…)

a draft version of your poem
a minimum of 6 and a maximum of 20 phrases
each phrase is on a new line
spelling has been checked
your evaluation sheet has been completed
you are on time

Student Total: /15   Teacher Total: /15

7 An Integrated Unit: Literature Circles to Promote Social Issues and Citizenship

Helping Students Understand Global Issues

During the autumn school term, we often ask students to report on stories in the news to familiarize them with reading the newspaper or listening to the news as well as speaking in class. In the past, the students tended to report the local atrocities — the more bizarre, the better. We intervened by stressing the importance of looking at events happening in international news. They then paraphrased the events outlined in the news article but often did not understand the major events underlying the story. We realized that our students have consistently lacked an understanding of the events, both past and present, that shape the world. How could we address these concerns within the constraints of the school year?

The impetus came from the resource teacher, who presented a list of novels she had read on the topics of immigration, war, and change. For our purposes, these novels represented examples of persecution. Some cases began in the past but continued today, while others were stories about current world events. The novels we selected dealt with a variety of issues, including war, immigration, alienation, and persecution. Our goal was to have students read novels that made them think about world issues that were, for the most part, beyond their own life experience.

The Unit

The novel selections were made after discussing specific student' needs as well as the motivational impact of these stories for eleven to thirteen year old students. We settled on seven titles reflecting historical events that had occurred in different parts of the world. Four copies of each of the following novels were initially chosen:

The Return — Sonia Levitin
Kiss the Dust — Elizabeth Laird
Year of Impossible Goodbyes — Sook Nyul Choi
Zlata's Diary — Zlata Filipovic
Days of Terror — Barbara Smucker
My Name is Seepeetza — Shirley Sterling
Goodbye, Vietnam — Gloria Whelan

Day One — Reading a Poem and Responding

To prepare the students for this unit, we began with discussions of a poem that dealt with the theme of war and alienation. We read the poem "Hiroshima Exit" by Joy Kogawa to the students. Next, the students reread the poem individually. For a third reading, the students were seated in groups and a student in each group read the poem aloud. Both during the teacher's reading of the poem and during the small-group reading, students were encouraged to draw, use a highlighter pen, or jot down ideas around the poem as they were listening. Afterwards, the students had a chance to ask specific questions about the poem.

For the questioning, we used a modified **ReQuest** procedure asking on-the-line, between-the-line, and beyond-the-line questions. Their questions often pertained to vocabulary and word meaning, but students would also ask about the tone of the poem. From there the students worked in their small groups to determine what the poem meant to them. Then they wrote a quick write (ten minutes) in response to the poem. These responses were shared with the larger group and served as the basis for later discussions in their literature groups once they began to read the novels. Notice the powerful harnessing of emotion with information evident in the two sample drafts.

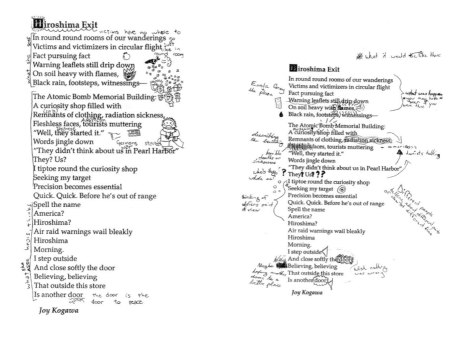

The poem "Hiroshima Exit" by Joy Kogawa appears twice with handwritten annotations:

Hiroshima Exit

In round round rooms of our wanderings
Victims and victimizers in circular flight
Fact pursuing fact
Warning leaflets still drip down
On soil heavy with flames,
Black rain, footsteps, witnessings—

The Atomic Bomb Memorial Building:
A curiosity shop filled with
Remnants of clothing, radiation sickness,
Fleshless faces, tourists muttering
"Well, they started it."
Words jingle down
"They didn't think about us in Pearl Harbor"
They? Us?
I tiptoe round the curiosity shop
Seeking my target
Precision becomes essential
Quick. Quick. Before he's out of range
Spell the name
America?
Hiroshima?
Air raid warnings wail bleakly
Hiroshima
Morning.
I step outside
And close softly the door
Believing, believing
That outside this store
Is another door

Joy Kogawa

Day Two — Introducing the Novels

The next step was to introduce each of the novels. We gave a short book
talk and then allowed the students time to peruse the novels that interested them. Selections were then made and the students were given
in-class time for reading. In assisting students who were not strong readers, we quietly suggested that they might like to try specific novels and
at that point guided them through a look at these novels (chapter or diary
format, main characters, setting, book jacket, and speculation about the
title) so they could make an informed decision about the title they
wanted to read.

What Happened

It was not surprising that most students did not understand the concept
of persecution since few of them had experienced this firsthand. It was
therefore necessary to explore their perceptions of persecution. Some of
the initial exploration was done through whole class discussions both
prior to reading and during the novel study. In our first discussion, when

the word *persecution* was used, some of the students had general ideas about the concept but others had no ideas. We then consulted a series of dictionaries, identifying the common ideas that were contained in the various definitions. Through this exercise, some of the students realized that the concept of persecution was broader than they had initially believed. The students then met in groups to predict how these ideas about persecution might impact on the characters in their novel. The students were then asked to record their thoughts about persecution using the clustering strategy, and a map of their thinking emerged.

This gave the students a starting point for their literature-group discussions about the persecution of the characters in their respective novels.

During class, the students met in literature groups to discuss questions and ideas they had while reading. Sometimes the literature groups were given discussion topics or activities to complete that were designed to further their understanding of the components of the novel. For example, one day the groups had to find evidence of conflict in their novel: person versus person, person versus self, and person versus nature. On another occasion, the students discussed the events leading up to and including the climax of the novel as well as the events surrounding the resolution. After each discussion, students wrote personal reflections in their response logs.

Two of the students with learning difficulties had chosen *Goodbye, Vietnam* and therefore were in the same literature group. One of the goals in each of these students' Individual Education Plans focused on the development of skills so that they could become more independent learners. This goal was especially important, because both students were moving to secondary school at the end of the year. In order to become more independent learners, both students needed to be able to comprehend their novels so that they could participate in the literature-group discussions and activities. Their reading comprehension problems necessitated helping them to draw connections between the main events and the characters in the novel. In this discussion group, we tried to involve the more-able readers in activities that reviewed the main ideas of the novel through retellings and story maps. We held individual conferences with the members of this group to ensure that all the students had an opportunity to discuss aspects of the novel that interested them. When a classroom assistant was available, the assistant would join this group in the teacher's stead.

Students used both in-class and at-home reading time to finish their novels. At the beginning of the unit, the class agreed that students should be able to read the novels as quickly as they desired. They also agreed that students who were reading ahead should not give away the story to those who had not read as far. Some students quickly read through most of the seven titles that were available. They then were able to choose which of the novels they wished to discuss and would join the literature groups accordingly. This kept group membership from being static. Students' progress was monitored on a poster on which the students' name appeared along with the titles of the novels and dates they completed reading each title. As a result, we sought out copies of additional novels that focused on war, immigration, alienation, and persecution. The novels we added to the collection were:

The Devil's Arithmetic — Jane Yolen
Taste of Salt — Frances Temple
The Old Brown Suitcase — Lillian Boraks-Nemetz
Anna Is Still Here — Ida Vos
The White Giraffe — Sook Nyul Choi
The Diary of Anne Frank — Anne Frank
Shabanu — Suzanne Fisher Staples
The Eternal Spring of Mr. Ito — Shiela Garrigue
Number the Stars — Lois Lowry

All of the literature groups completed a **Sociogram**, in which students discussed words to describe the personalities of the characters as well as to compare the relationships between the characters. Students discussed two of the main characters from their novel. They recorded words that described each character's personality and included them in a Venn diagram. After everyone's ideas were added to the diagram, the students then began to discuss the relationship between these two characters. They tried to find words to describe the relationship and used two-ended arrows to show if it was an attribute that was true for each of the characters. One-ended arrows were used when the attribute only pertained to one of the characters. All the group members participated in visually representing these ideas on poster paper. Alex's example, using *The Diary of Anne Frank*, demonstrates the relationship of key characters.

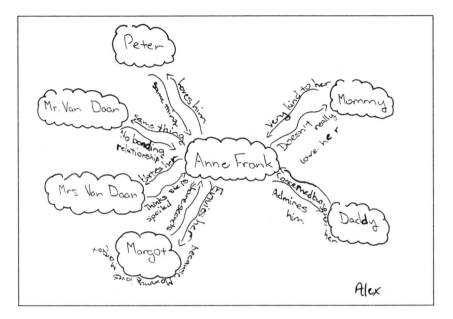

This activity often generated lively discussion as the students tried to think of words to describe the personalities and relationships between the various characters. The teacher's role was to move in and out of these discussions, guiding groups when they needed some support, listening as the students were reading passages as evidence to support their points of view, or encouraging students to continue to return to the text for evidence to support their opinions.

Another activity that was completed by the literature groups was an **Ideagram**, or **Visual Cluster**. This activity involved students providing evidence to show how a particular character was persecuted. The evidence would be in the form of:

- visual representations from the text: drawings, magazine photos or other pictures,
- quotations from the text,
- connections to real world events portrayed in the media.

A series of rings was drawn around the topic of persecution. In the ring next to the topic, the students could include pictorial examples of persecution taken from the novel, quotations from the novel that demonstrated the persecution of a character. In the outer ring, students were to look for connections in the media and other sources that proved persecution of a group of people had occurred.

Since updates pertaining to the war in the former Yugoslavia figured prominently in the media at the time of this literature study, many of the students investigated this as an example of persecution based on ethnic and religious differences. The posters were completed by small groups of students within the literature groups. These, too, generated a great deal of discussion.

Evaluation — Pencil and Paper, and Beyond

We evaluated the Ideagrams using the following four-point scale. Student self-evaluation was followed by teacher evaluation. Usually, there is little difference between the student/teacher scoring.

We want to monitor the comprehension skills of students in ways other than pencil and paper activities. This enables students to use and develop alternate ways of showing their understanding of a novel. It is also fairer to those students who comprehend well but are not particularly fluent in written response.

Since character development had been one of the focuses of the literature-group discussions, we were interested to know how much the students had learned about the characters from their reading and their discussion groups. A **Hot Seat** would require individual students to select a specific character from any one of the novels they had read, research this character, and respond, in role, to questions about his or her life.

Criteria for Persecution Ideagrams

4 variety of visual representations
several quotations from the text
voice, personal opinion, or reflection on persecution
connections to other books, news, stories
emotional connection evident

3 variety of visual representations
only one quotation
personal opinion or emotional connections apparent but not developed
some connections

2 visual representation not fully explored
no personal opinion or emotional connection
few, if any, connections
few, if any, quotations

1 limited response, few connections

Once the students had selected a character, they wrote a biography of that character, including information on the character's major achievements, personal and family information, ethnic group, birthplace/where they lived, religion, and the kinds of persecution they experienced. To complete this biography the students reread parts of the novel, consulted atlases and CD-ROM encyclopedias to clarify geographical questions they had, and conferenced with other students for clarification. After their peers had edited their first drafts, the students each produced a copy of their biography as an overhead transparency.

In preparation for the Hot Seat, students wrote down questions for their character while others in their literature circle helped formulate answers to their questions. This gave all students a chance to practise thinking and answering the kinds of questions that could be asked in the presentation. Here is an example of a series of questions and answers for Annemarie from *Number the Stars*.

On the day of their Hot Seat presentation, the students were to be in character when they sat down in front of the audience. Some students even planned costumes, hairstyles, or hats to help be in character. The student on the hot seat placed their overhead transparency on the overhead projector so that the audience could read them. This information remained on screen so that the audience could ask specific questions based on the background information supplied. The overhead also

Kiss the Dust

Dana   *Jan. 24, 1996*

name - Tara Hawrami
age - thirteen years old.
family members - Kak Soran, Teriska
Khan, Hero and Gelti.
birthplace/where I live/lived Sulaimaniya
Iraq; Teheran, Iran; London.
ethnic group - Kurd.
religion - less - traditional Muslim
That means, I don't usually go
to mosque (church) but I sometime
do pray.
major achievements:
- going to school, being a good
  student and having lots of friends.
- crossing the mountains to Iran
- going on a plane to London
- starting school in London.
persecution:
- having to flee from my home
  land because the secret police were
  after my dad.
- leaving my school, my bestfriend
  and my house
- having their village bombed
- being a Kurd. and a muslim.

HOT SEAT : The Return

<u>Name</u> - Desta

<u>Age</u> - I don't know and I don't count how old I am like the rest of my family.

<u>Family Members</u> - Aunt Kibret, Uncle Teckle, Almaz, and Joas

<u>Ethnic Group</u> - African

<u>Where I Live</u> - Ethiopia, Africa and later I moved to Jerusalem

<u>Religion</u> - Jewish

<u>Major Achievements</u> - Escaping Ethiopia and moving to Jerusalem.

I was religiously persecuted so I left Ethiopia.

assisted the students who had not read all of the novels. After reading the information on the overhead, most students then formulated questions for the student on the hot seat.

Initially, we were concerned that the audience might not ask any questions, making it uncomfortable for the student on the hot seat. To counteract this tendency, the students were told that a tally of the number of "thoughtful" questions that were asked would be kept. As a class, we determined what a thoughtful question might sound like, and during the first few presentations we modeled these questions by asking several questions of each presenter. After receiving the answer, the class would be asked if they thought the criteria for a thoughtful question had been met. If they decided not, advice was given on how to make the question more thoughtful. Keeping track of their questions greatly motivated the audience, which in turn inspired the student on the hot seat to formulate good answers from the character's point of view.

Each student's progress was recorded using the criteria the class had generated. The class had developed these criteria in a meeting that had occurred prior to the presentations, so all the students were aware of how they would be evaluated.

The presentations were spaced out over several days so that the students did not tire of the activity. Perhaps this precaution was unnecessary, because the majority of students indicated their desire to complete another hot seat presentation after all the students had participated. We used two different data collections for evaluating student progress. First, we kept notes on each presentation, both the oral responses as well as the written biography. Second, we tallied the number of thoughtful questions asked and point notes outlining specifics about the questions. We shared both of these sheets with the students when the hot seat presentations were complete.

HOT SEAT EVALUATION

Name_____

BODY LANGUAGE

4	3	2	1
Body language and facial expressions fit the character's mood very well	Most of the body language and facial expressions fit the character's mood	Some of the body language fits the character. Some facial expressions are used	Very little of the body language or facial expressions fit the character's mood

ACCURACY OF ANSWERS

The answers are always detailed, thoughtful and fit the character	Most answers are accurate, thoughtful and detailed	Some of the answers are thoughtful and detailed but some do not include detailed information	Few of the answers contain detail and some of the answers confuse the audience

PRESENTATION

Presentation is very neat and clear. Spelling or grammatical mistakes are not noticeable	Few spelling or grammatical errors are present and they do not distract the reader. Presentation is clear	Some distracting errors are present. It is difficult to read the overhead	Lots of errors are present. The overhead is very difficult to read (words may be deleted, and printing is unclear)

CLARITY OF VOICE

A clear, expressive voice is used which projects to the back of the room. The person is able to stay in character	The voice can be heard and a fair amount of expression is used. Generally stays in character	The voice is difficult to hear at times and it lacks expression. From time to time the person is not in character	Voice is almost impossible to hear. No expression is evident and the person is not able to stay in character

ACCURACY OF INFORMATION ON OVERHEAD

All information is accurate and there are many supporting details	Most of the information is accurate and there are quite a few details given	Lacks accurate information. Very few details are provided	Very little information is provided overall. There are obvious mistakes in the information given

TOTAL/20

COMMENTS

A Final Activity — Making a Back-Pocket Journal

We planned a final activity during this unit to make the students more aware of ways to help the victims of persecution. During the unit, Professor Emile Tanay, a Croatian art educator who has been working with Croatian and Bosnian children traumatized by the war in the former Yugoslavia, spoke in the city. In his presentation, he introduced the children he has been working with through their stories and their art. The images and themes in the children's artwork were frightening. When discussing this in class, our students were eager to reach out and contact the children in Bosnia and Croatia.

Thus our culminating project would be hand-bound notebooks with blue jean covers.

Each student prepared the paper notebooks, covered them with jean material, and then decorated the outside books with embroidery, paints, buttons, and other innovations. Most of the students included pencils and other writing materials within pockets they made in the jean material. Each bookmaker personalized the book for its recipient with a short poem using peace as the theme and included a photo of the bookmaker. The students were very proud of their book designs. A local radio station agreed to pay for the postage to send the books to Professor Tanay.

The books were then packaged for mailing and sent. A week after the books were mailed, the class reflected on what they had learned about persecution. Some of the students' written reflections are included here.

In Conclusion — The Development of Citizenship

Our goal of assisting students in developing a better understanding of the events, past and present, that shape our world was being realized in their responses to the persecution unit. We had moved well beyond the superficial hype—with no personal connection—of their initial reports on the news. We have repeated this unit on several occasions. Always, the powerful learning of all the students, and their desire to take action to match their thinking, humbles us. This, we believe, is the development of citizenship.

Making a Back-Pocket Journal*

1. Use standard 81/2 x 11 inch paper.
2. Cut in half on a paper cutter to 81/2 x 51/2.
3. Make sections by folding 4 sheets in half into 51/2 x 41/4.
   - can use decorated sheets on the outside of each section
   - can make a title page with the first page of the first section
4. Use as many of these sections as needed to make the journal (4 make a 32 page book, 6 make 48 pages).
5. Rip leg of the blue jean, making the seam at the centre to be the book spine about 6 x 11 or 12 inches (depends on how much foldover you want).
   - can leave space to hold pen or pencil
6. Wrap cover around book and secure with elastic so that it won't slip when you are putting in the holes.
7. Place on block of wood and put in 3 holes about 1/2 inch in from the spine with a hammer and nail.
   - 3-hole binding, holes at 1, 3, 5
   - 5-hole binding, holes at 1, 2, 3, 4, 5
8. Do oriental binding starting at the centre hole and going around the head and foot.
9. Glue down the edges of the fabric and leave space for the back cover to turn over the edge and secure book.
10. Attach Velcro™ to secure cover.

*Courtesy of Anne Vicente, Vancouver Teacher and Artist.

Persecution

I now know that persecution is a large problem in every society, including ours. My concern is that this will never really stop and it seems to me that very few notice this. To make a difference I want to reach out to the helpless as I grow to my adult years. I want to be a father figure to those that don't have fathers because of wars that are caused by their ethnic background. I wish I could say I knew how much it hurts for these people but I can't because I have no similar situations. I hope everybody would take a stand and see these problems and try their hardest to change them. This is my wish.

Ben

I am aware that persecution is one of the most awful things in the world. I myself have experienced persecution many times because of the fact that my skin is not white. People have said that my skin looks like things that I would rather no write about. I don't even want to think about it. I am also aware of the fact that persecution is not just about different races and religious beliefs, it has to do with much more than that. I also know now that persecution happens to a lot more people than I thought.

I am concerned that persecution will never stop and that there will be wars started by it. It really scares me. It scares me that persecution could destroy us. Wars could have destroyed people from the Early Ages (e.g. Cro-Magnon) or people like the Maya. If persecution can start wars and wars can destroy people, I am very afraid that persecution can destroy us.

I think that the jean books we made to send to the Bosnian children helped make a little bit of a difference, not that much, but it was still something. It really showed that people do care for each other. I think that if everyone showed that they cared, that a very big difference can be made. I'm not too sure about the other things that I can do right now, but I think that caring is one of the most important factors because showing caring may be able to give people that are persecuted the strength and the hope to fight persecution.

By Amita

Persecution, what is the true meaning of that? Is it the act of hurting or harming another? I have learned a lot from the studies we have done over the year and now, I have much, much more respect for other races. Racism is a big part of persecution. A way we can help is to think that everybody is one race. Although we have some differences, we can help each other and make it a better world. To show empathy to the people you treat badly and think what they would feel is a good way to help too. Persecuting others doesn't do any good, but it will hurt people's feelings and make a place of terror. People afraid of you and doing whatever you say is not right. The right way is to help others, gain respect and people will help you anyway. It doesn't matter if you are rich or poor, we all live on the same planet and we should help each other. Thank you.

Geoffrey

8 Science/Ecology — Working with the Eight Intelligences

Broadening the Means of Scientific Communication

One of the goals of an intermediate science curriculum is to provide students with opportunities to learn to communicate scientifically. Too often, this scientific communication is translated in the classroom as the lab write-up following an experiment that has been demonstrated to the students. Students are taught to record the procedures, observations, and conclusions in a prescribed manner; their ability to correctly explain the scientific principles is used as evidence of their ability to communicate scientifically. That real scientists do not necessarily communicate their findings in this way tends to be overlooked.

In seeking a framework to broaden the means by which scientific knowledge could be communicated, we examined Gardner's theory of **Multiple Intelligences** (Fogarty, Robin. *Problem-Based Learning and Other Curriculum Models for the Multiple Intelligences Classroom.* Arlington Heights, Illinois: IRI Skylight, 1997). In multiple-intelligence theory, there are eight ways of learning. These intelligences are:

- verbal-linguistic
- logical-mathematical
- visual-spatial
- musical

- bodily-kinesthetic
- naturalist
- interpersonal
- intrapersonal

Using this theory, a student's intelligence is seen as the product of her or his ability to communicate knowledge and understanding of the world through any number of these intelligences. The science lab write-up was evidence of linguistic intelligence and perhaps logical-mathematical intelligence, but it did not begin to tap the other intelligences that scientists must develop to communicate in a variety of situations. A scientist also uses bodily-kinesthetic intelligence, which is the ability to process knowledge through a process such as an experiment. Spatial intelligence is used when designing an experiment and then explaining it to others using illustrations. When scientists must present their work to others to secure a position, grant, or funding, they require interpersonal intelligence. Scientists often work in research teams that necessitate strong intrapersonal intelligence. Finally, the naturalist intelligence demonstrates an understanding of the physical world, of ecosystems, and the connectedness in nature. It became clear that to reach the goal of teaching students to communicate scientifically, we needed to provide opportunities for the students to develop a repertoire of skills integrating these intelligences.

In planning the Ecology component of the Life Sciences unit in the grades 6 and 7 science curriculum, our primary learning objective was to enhance students' ability to communicate scientifically. Our activities had to allow students to build their knowledge and then demonstrate it, in a variety of ways. This would enable students for whom English was a Second Language to build their understanding through a variety of experiences, not just reading and writing. Students who thrived on open-ended exploration would have no ceiling placed on their participation. The tasks in which they were engaged should allow them to plan and design unique ways to build and then communicate their knowledge. Students who experienced academic difficulties could prove to be very powerful learners in a different setting. They too could demonstrate understanding through their learning strengths.

Building Background Information

The science concepts taught throughout this unit are outlined in the following web of topics. To teach these concepts, we designed lessons that involve students in a variety of group activities. Whenever possible, the students investigated news stories and magazine articles that allowed them to discuss the complexities of issues surrounding the environment. They realized that easy answers to these problems were not always possible or plausible.

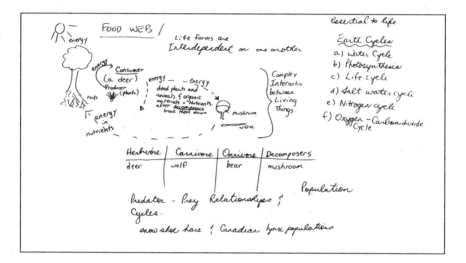

Once the students understood the concepts that were the backbone of the unit, we planned a fieldtrip to develop their observational skills in the outdoors. With the assistance of park naturalists, we designed a program to involve the students in various outdoor activities that would show them how different life forms found in the forest are interdependent on one other. We discovered how to be observant and notice birds who were feeding on insects that lived in the crevices of tree bark, as well as to notice different types of fungi and insects living on the fallen "nurse" logs that littered the forest floor. Here, the food web became more than a flowchart for the students, since they could now see how all the species were interdependent in a food web. The naturalists reinforced the vocabulary that had been learned throughout the unit, which demonstrated to the students how these words were used everyday by biologists in communicating with others.

Evaluation — Multiple Representations of Understanding

A written test at the end of the unit would not accurately assess the students' ability to communicate scientifically. We wanted to assess their ability to successfully communicate scientific knowledge, individually and as members of a team. We wanted to be more broad based in our assessment and encourage multiple representations of understandings. We also required an individual essay.

The teacher-librarian had assisted us in planning this unit. During our library times, we often co-taught the lessons. In planning our summative assessment, the teacher librarian, the resource teacher, and the classroom teacher sat down together to brainstorm possibilities. We all agreed that the students would integrate the information they had learned in the unit if they had the opportunity to further investigate a local ecosystem. We carefully structured a group assignment to deepen the understanding of all the students.

Working in teams, the students would look for signs of insect, plants, and animals that would inhabit such ecosystems as the seashore, pond, estuary, river, forest, or creek. While in this ecosystem, students would record their findings using a combination of lists, photographs, video recordings, observational notes, and drawings. After they had completed their group visits, the students would work together to construct a diorama of their ecosystem using a large box as the structural support for their display. Students would be encouraged to use nonliving items from nature as well as items made of clay, Plasticine™, or other craft supplies. The school's art specialist would give the students a workshop on the construction of dioramas with suggestions for different ways they could be designed.

The evaluation would have to be both group and individual. We wanted to assess how well the team had worked together to achieve their goal of communicating in a scientific way what they had learned about their ecosystem. This evaluation would be of the diorama, requiring strengths in the visual-spatial, interpersonal, bodily-kinesthetic, and naturalist intelligences. Each student would also be required to write an essay. This would be a more traditional evaluation, the product or the essay requiring strengths in both verbal-linguistic (the writing) and logical-mathematical intelligences (following a prescribed format). The processes for collecting this information, however, would have crossed many of the intelligences.

We decided that each student in the group would identify and

Use the following format as a guide for the write-up about the organism that you chose for your part of the Interdependence Project.

PARAGRAPH 1
- topic sentence that introduces the essay subject
- identify the organism that has been studied
- include the Latin and common names (if both can be found)
- tell whether your organism is a predator or prey

PARAGRAPH 2
- location of the organism
- describe the ecosystem, niche, climate and biogeoclimatic zone where your organism lives and finds shelter
- describe the other organisms that live in this ecosystem

PARAGRAPH 3
- explain how the organism fits into the Food Web
- describe and provide evidence if the organism is a herbivore, carnivore or omnivore
- explain how the organism is interdependent on other organisms

PARAGRAPH 4
- describe changes in the ecosystem that have occurred or are still occurring
- describe problems which this organism has to face
- describe the adaptations, if any, the organism has made to survive

PARAGRAPH 5
- summarize the main ideas of your essay
- describe what needs to be done to protect this organism
- describe what must be done to protect the ecosystem where it lives
- leave the reader with an idea of something that they could do to assist in protecting the biodiversity in our local ecosystems

Length: No longer than 2 word-processed pages or 4 double-spaced, handwritten pages.

Bibliography: Include all sources and follow the format in the library.

research a different plant, insect, bird, or animal that would be found in their ecosystem so that they could then write a two-page essay. We gave the students a structured outline (follows) for the essay. This provided tremendous support for those students who required it, and prevented direct copying from text. Students needed to take notes, re-form them, and then write with their own voice. The requirements for the paragraphs in this outline also encouraged student to use several sources to complete their research.

Each of the organisms chosen by the members of the group were to be included in the diorama as a part of a food web illustrating how the organisms were dependent on other organisms within the ecosystem. The conversations that occurred during the group field study, as well as during the construction of the diorama, greatly increased their understanding of the ecological concepts. In addition, the required use of specific vocabulary in the essay made the students aware that in order to communicate to their audience they required a working understanding of the concepts about which they were writing.

To evaluate the projects, the students brainstormed all the components of the dioramas and of the essays that they thought were important to consider. At this point, we helped the students to organize these ideas into categories for ease of evaluation. We also added criteria that we felt, as teachers, were important. We explained our reasons for including these criteria. The students' criteria and rating scale follow. These were posted and the teams polished their dioramas against these criteria before moving to the 'team evaluation' process.

The students remained in the groups they had formed for the project during the evaluation, since they were used to working together. Each group was given one of the criteria in which to evaluate; for example, Kim's group was assigned "Diorama, Realistic Representation." In each group, the students discussed how they would allot the ten possible points each project could earn. Thus Kim's group saw all of the team's projects and assigned them a score out of 10 for "Diorama, Realistic Representation." This process occurred in the library with the teacher librarian. Having two teachers in the room enabled us to circulate to each of the groups, offering suggestions about their evaluation techniques and encouraging them to refer specifically to the criteria they had developed.

As teachers, we reviewed the marks assigned by the student teams.

CRITERIA USED FOR GROUP EVALUATION
OF THE ECOSYSTEM PROJECTS

1. Bibliography

5	4	3	2	1
Included 3+ sources in alphabetical order. No errors were evident and all punctuation was included. Used correct format.	Also included 3+ sources in order. Few mistakes were made so the reader is not distracted. Punctuation and format are correct.	Used fewer than 3 sources. Errors are noticeable in either spelling or punctuation but they generally do not distract the reader. Small changes made to the format.	Fewer than three sources were used. Punctuation errors are evident. Names are not in alphabetical order. Errors distract the reader. Format errors are noticeable.	One source was used and lots of errors are present. The format changes for each source.

2. Conventions of Writing

Sentences are very fluent. No mistakes are evident. Detailed and on-topic paragraphing. No run-on-sentences.	Few spelling and punctuation errors. Good sentences and few run-on sentences.	Some spelling and punctuation errors. Some run-on sentences. Good paragraphing.	Many errors in punctuation and spelling. Needs work on paragraphing.	A lot of mistakes in text. Not all paragraphs completed.

3. DIORAMA – Artist's Interpretation

Almost looks real. Colourful and detailed with no loose ends. Creative design is evident in the ecosystem and food web.	Quite realistic with few loose ends. Quite a colourful effect with good attention to detail and design.	A few loose ends. Fairly detailed. Ecosystem and food web are included but they are not the focus of the diorama.	Very few details. Several loose ends are evident. The ecosystem and food web are included but they provide little information.	Looks like a box. Lacks colour and creativity. Ecosystem and food web are confusing. Items are falling off. The diorama seems incomplete.

4. DIORAMA – Realistic Representation

Realistic drawings, and natural items were used. Background clear and realistic. The outside of the box is very well done, with lots of clear photos, pictures, drawings and labels.	Included some realistic drawings and natural items. Interesting ways were used to show the ecosystem.	Few realistic drawings were used for the background. Few natural items used. One or two clear drawings showing the ecosystem were included.	Partially finished background. The box still looks like a box. Lacks clear drawings of the ecosystem. Very few natural items used.	No detailed drawings for the background were included. Lacked natural items. Photos, labels, and drawings are not clear.

5. FOOD WEB

Lots of information included. Very clear labels and connections. Overall presentation is excellent.	Most information included. Connections shown. Good labels, and clear information.	Labels are fairly clear but not very eyecatching. Lacks sufficient information.	Labels are not clear. Connections are not shown.	Visually confusing to the audience. No connections are shown.

6. SUBTOPICS

All topics of the outline are included. Information is written in the author's words. Interesting and varied sentences explain the information clearly.	Most topics included. Sentences are easily understood so the reader isn't distracted.	Several topics included. Information is fairly clear and understandable.	Very few topics included. Sentences are poorly developed. Information is not presented clearly.	Only one topic is included. Sentences are not informative because information is scarce.

7. SCIENTIFIC VOCABULARY

All terms used correctly, in detailed and interesting sentences.	Most terms used in good sentences but no Latin name was included.	Half of the terms used in quite well developed sentences.	Few terms were used. Some words are not correctly used in sentences.	None of the terms were used correctly in sentences.

Few adjustments were required, as the students were very clear about the expectations for success. We then collected the individual essays and marked them for scientific content, using the following scale. (The student teams had already evaluated them for scientific vocabulary, subtopics, conventions of writing, and bibliography.) This was a weighted scale — we judged out of 5, then multiplied by 4, giving a possible total of 20.

---

5 The student has exceeded the expectations, demonstrating insight and creativity.

4 The student has successfully met all of the criteria.

3 The student has met most of the criteria.

2 The student has met only some of the criteria.

1 The task was inappropriate for the student at this time.

Throughout this process, students were able to read and see the projects produced by other students in the class. When they saw the range of ways to complete the project, they gained new ideas for tackling future assignments. The evaluation process gave students a chance to witness how a subjective evaluation is completed. Some of the groups' debates on how to score particular projects were very illuminating for us as teachers. In most of the cases, it was evident that the students valued the same things that we do when evaluating their work. The students had fun, experienced a great deal of success, learned a lot of science, and moved their learning outside the traditional boundaries of the classroom. The following two essays are samples of how all students could participate with success in this unit.

Raccoon   By: Lindsay

Have you ever shooed away a raccoon eating your garbage? Next time that you see one, stop and watch it for awhile. You will see that raccoons are very misunderstood. Raccoons are very playful creatures and they are not trying to upset humans. The fact that they have adapted to city life and are not afraid of humans is not their fault at all. Raccoons are consumers. They eat other things. So why are they living in the center of the city? This and much more will be answered in this report.

The raccoon is an omnivore. This means they eat a variety of different things. Some of the raccoons favorite foods are: crayfish, fish, frogs, garbage, mice and squirrels. The raccoon also eats things that are already dead and some plants. Because most things raccoons eat live in the water, they like to live where there is fresh water nearby. There is not a lot of things that eat raccoons but since they live near the city, the raccoon population is kept down by people in cars and the fact that they are not protected. Some things that do eat raccoons are: cougars, bears, wolves and other big cats. Most of these animals prefer to eat the babies.

The raccoon lives in the forest. They live in cavities in trees, ditches in the ground and other sheltered areas. Raccoons are not very picky about their location but since they like to live near water, they usually don't live very high up in the mountains. They also can't survive in very, very cold climates like the Yukon. Most raccoons don't care about what kind of forests they live in as long as they have all of the above. This is probably why they like Vancouver so much. The fact is, they are not living in the city, we are living in the forest. If you think about it, raccoons have probably been living in Vancouver for hundreds of years. Then we decided to build our city right in the middle of the forest. For example, the North shore mountains, Stanley Park and Pacific Spirit Park were all here before us and were all homes for raccoons. Now raccoons have decided to live in city parks because we took down so much of their habitat.

A raccoon's life cycle is very simple. They are considered babies for around two years. For the first year, they stay in their homes almost all of the time. They live on their mothers milk for only about six months. When they are two years old, they can leave their homes but they usually stay close to their mothers for the first month. Baby raccoons are very playful and curious. This is how most baby raccoons are hurt or killed. They sometimes might wander on to a busy road without their mothers seeing and end up badly injured. Raccoons in zoos can live up to about fifteen years but in the wild they live about only twelve years because of the amount of dangers.

Some drastic changes that have happened in the raccoons ecosystem are clear cutting, highways and toxic garbage. Raccoons are now used to traffic and people but they don't always remember about cars when they are crossing the road. They have become so used to roads being there that they don't consider them being a threat. One major change in the ecosystem is that the forest is being cut down rapidly. This is why raccoons are not living in parks, riverbeds and even peoples backyards. Another threat to raccoons is that if people throw away some fish and toxic garbage in the same bag, the raccoons might eat the poison and get sick or die.

So next time you see a raccoon, watch it and learn. Try to be careful not to throw away toxins and food in the same bag and learn to care about the forest. We protect our homes from burglars but raccoons can't protect the forest against us.

Cat Tails   Byron

The cat tail has two names one is called a cat tail and the other name is bull rush. Some people and a lot of books call it a cat tail because at the end of the brown round part it looks like it has a tail. The cat tails have flat leaves about an inch wide. They have a strong stem that grows high. Four quarters of the way up is a dark brown and oval shape, which is part of the cat tail. The cat tail contains pollen grains and just above it is a little tip that looks like a tail. The Latin name for cat tails if Typha Latifotia. This organism is prey for Red Wing Black birds and Muskrats. The organism is a provider for the Red Wing Black birds and the Muskrats.

This organism is located in estuaries in Vancouver and Richmond and many other places. I saw them in Terra Nova next to the river – there are thousands of them growing free. Cat tails live in many different climates including those which get snow to heat. It lives in very swampy waters, but has no shelter from rain. A lot of dead tree bark is in the area where they live.

The cat tails fit into the food web when Red Wing Black birds or Muskrats take the pollen for food. Then they die in the years and make better soil which the cat tails use to survive. When the snow geese come near winter they drop their droppings and that is good for the soil too. Cat tails are Herbivores because they use soil to survive not meat or both. If there was no soil or animals there would not be any cat tails.

There is less room for them to grow because they took up all the room in the beginning of Terra Nova and in other places I think is the same. It is also facing pollution because you drive right up to where they are when you go for a walk. To survive, the dark brown just before the tip turns into fluff to spread to make more cat tails in years to come.

To protect the cat tails we should give them more room to grow, move them away from the pollution and we will see many more. To protect where it lives there should not be any cars around so that it can live without pollution. No one should litter because it is hard for them to live with all the garbage so throw it in the garbage bins.

9 Computer Buddies: Researching with HyperCard and the Internet

Learning the Basics of Computer Programming

Computer technology has evolved to the point that the majority of new students arriving at school already know basic computer skills. Even in the primary levels, most students have learned to use a mouse-activated drawing program and many even use a "hunt and peck" method of typing with good accuracy. Their computer skills have developed through the purchase of home computers that have greatly increased their access to computer technology. In the mid to late 1980s, it was usual to expect that students had little experience with a computer outside the school environment. During this period, it was acceptable to base the computer curriculum on exploration of the computer focusing on word-processing skills, computer drawing, and basic computer operation. With the burgeoning computer market and the technological advances occurring in this field, students are now ready for more-challenging experiences in their computer classes. That schools, for the most part, are unable to update their computer hardware with the frequency that many families are able to afford makes designing a computer curriculum that is relevant and meaningful to our students somewhat challenging for teachers.

In the last few years, students and teachers have been utilizing our Macintosh™ computers in unique ways. We have discovered the power of **HyperCard**, a software program for Macintosh computers. This program has enabled students from grades 1 through 7 to learn the basics and the complexities of computer programming. Rather than providing our students with more time to explore software that they might already use at home, we decided they might be motivated to learn how to use computer language to design their own programs. Our project was initially developed to help integrate students with physical disabilities into the classroom through the use of computer technology. What really happened was our discovery of a most powerful learning tool for all the students in the school. The teachers have become learners, as our students teach us the intricacies of computer programming.

The Plan — Burning Questions

After replacing our aging computer lab with sixteen brand-new Macintosh computers, teachers and parents were voicing concern about how the lab was being used by students. True, we did have computers that were loaded with a variety of educational games that the students delighted in playing during their computer classes, but even with the addition of word-processing programs, we felt that the students were not expanding their knowledge of computer skills. We had even been noticing that students were tending to become bored playing our limited number of computer programs. At this point, several teachers began to take courses offered through our school district to learn more about the HyperCard program and to expand our computer skills. We found local workshops for Macintosh computer users as well as a school-district-wide Macintosh Users Group, an ad hoc group of teachers who gave short workshops, discussed issues, and tried out new computer software and hardware.

The HyperCard program is simply a means of writing your own computer program without the prerequisite of being a technological whiz. When we first learned how to use HyperCard, the instructors never referred to what we were doing as "computer programming"; instead, we were designing "HyperCard stacks." This was done intentionally to prevent us from panicking at the thought of embarking on something as complicated as computer programming. We learned to draw, make buttons, and to tell the computer how to organize our cards — in short, we were programming the computer. These groups provided confidence for us to explore the computer as something more than a tool for word processing.

The initial reaction of we teachers to the HyperCard program was that it was an exciting, if not a bit confusing, way of getting the computer to do the things we wanted. In early lessons, we learned the tools to do simple animated sequences with personal cartoon characters. Later, we learned how to design the interior of a basic house plan and by using a series of buttons, maneuver from room to room in the design. As we were learning these skills, we taught them to the students in grades 6 and 7. They were very motivated to learn these skills. Their experience of the computer up to that point had been one of interacting with preprogrammed software packages. Now they could make the computer do what they wanted! We gingerly mastered the skills; the students leaped ahead. It was apparent that they were eagerly learning to make sense of a very powerful learning tool. To support our learning we also used *The Complete HyperCard 2.0 Handbook* (Goodman, Danny. New York: Random House, 1990).

Once the students had mastered the basics of HyperCard (animation, sound production, graphics, and text), we needed to decide how the program was to be used in our computer curriculum. That we had learned the basics just ahead of our students meant we hadn't thought as much about curricular considerations because we were just beginning to understand the capabilities of the program ourselves. We were aware that the students were at the point where they would learn more about HyperCard if given the opportunity to explore the program through teaching others. At our school, each class has a "buddy class." We decided that our grade 1 buddies were an excellent starting point for the grade 6/7 students. Both our class and the buddy class included students with a variety of special educational needs, including students with physical disabilities, intellectual disabilities, behavioural problems, and students for whom English was a second language.

Since our computer lab has only sixteen computers, students needed to develop the ability to cooperatively work with others. Modeling cooperative behaviour while developing computer skills were our overall goals for the students, but we needed an authentic task so that both student age groups would be sufficiently motivated to become engaged in this process. We began with a bulletin board of Burning Questions that the students had generated. Our plan was then to involve the younger students in asking the older students to help them solve their burning question through research. Their goal would be to display their learning in a HyperCard format. The grade 6/7 students had previously completed a number of library research projects, but this would be different.

Not only were they being asked to research a topic they were also required to assist a younger student in understanding how to answer a question. This necessitated that the older students use all that they had learned about research and to teach it to someone younger and less academically skilled than themselves.

Prior to the first meeting of the classes, the primary teacher worked with his class to determine what questions his students wanted to answer. For students who had difficulty with this task, books of questions were discussed. We carefully matched students to optimize the development of successful partnerships. In several groups, this necessitated having three students working together instead of two. We found that, with the younger students, same-gender groupings sometimes allowed for smoother working relationships. The partners were then put into one of two working groups led by the teachers. These groups would meet for a double period of eighty minutes once each week.

Using HyperCard to Present a Topic

During the first forty minutes together, one-half of the group would meet in the library while the other group met in the computer lab. The teacher-librarian assisted the library group in narrowing topics, locating material, and completing research. As students recorded facts, they wrote down the information on recipe-sized cards. This was done to concretely represent the idea of "cards" in a HyperCard "stack." The students then glued the cards into topics and subtopics following a **Mind Map** organizational format.

After forty minutes, the groups would switch, with the library group taking their information to the computer lab and the group in the computer lab moved to the library. Usually we presented a mini-lesson on the use of the HyperCard toolbar to the students in the computer room. Following this, the students worked on the computers to develop their project.

All the students designed a title page for their stack that included the name of their topic as well as the authors' names. Often these title pages were made more interesting with the addition of sound or animation. The next card in the sequence tended to be a table of contents, which was similar to the organization of the recipe cards in the mind map. Each topic that was included in the table of contents was made into a

HyperCard "button," which was directly linked to cards that provided more information about that subtopic. For example, in the HyperCard stack about the planet Saturn, the table of contents included subtopics such as Saturn's rings, what the rings are made of, and a quiz to check the audience's understanding of what they had learned after viewing the stack. Clicking one of these buttons led to a card explaining that Saturn's rings are made up of debris, small rocks, and sand. In this way, a browser could access the information he or she wanted to learn in the order that made sense rather than in a predetermined order of presentation.

Once the students had learned how to use animation and sound, they were motivated to integrate these special effects into their stacks. Some students taped their own voices using the computer's microphone while others used prerecorded sounds from the HyperCard "Sounds a Plenty" library. To achieve some of the animated effects that the students developed required that they learn to use HyperTalk, the language for programming, or "scripting," as it is known in HyperCard. Quickly it became evident that the students were learning to use the lexicon of HyperTalk in an intuitive way. Rather than experiencing difficulty with this new language, the students were quickly able to remember the basic commands and were eager to learn what happened when new commands were added. In fact, some students acquired books on HyperCard and began to learn advanced scripting at a rate that far surpassed their teachers! These students became instructors who taught the rest of the groups mini-lessons in scripting. Students who were ready to explore these skills excelled once they had peers whom they could approach with their questions. At this point, we realized that the project had truly become student centered.

Adaptations

As students and teachers gained experience with HyperCard, we began looking for new challenges. We still used the Goodman resource and built many mini-lessons from it. In this scenario, we were looking at a grade 6/7 and a grade 3 buddy class. Since most of the students learned these new skills quickly, we were able to focus on developing the social skills required for successful collaboration.

We continued with the Burning Question project while extending the

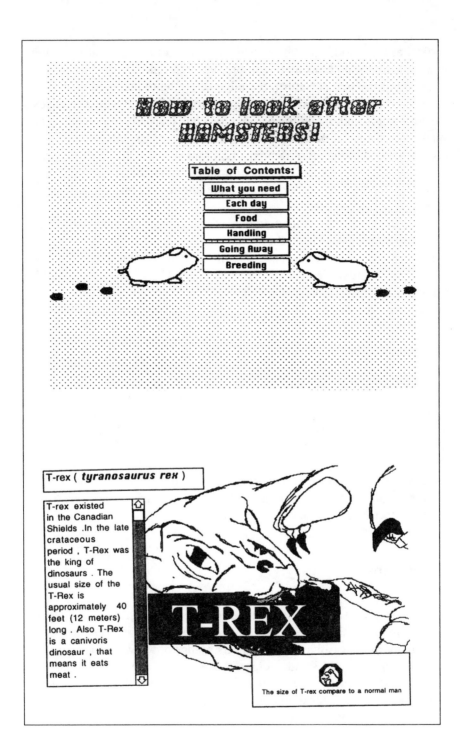

How to look after HAMSTERS!

Table of Contents:

T-rex (*tyranosaurus rex*)

T-rex existed in the Canadian Shields .In the late crataceous period , T-Rex was the king of dinosaurs . The usual size of the T-Rex is approximately 40 feet (12 meters) long . Also T-Rex is a canivoris dinosaur , that means it eats meat .

T-REX

The size of T-rex compare to a normal man

skills of the students. As each year begins, we now find that some students have worked extensively with HyperCard, while others have had no experience with it. This certainly adds to the diversity in any given class. To provide practice and to develop their skills, the older students designed a haunted house. This project used buttons to link a variety of cards, each featuring a room in the house. Students could participate in this activity at whatever level of ability they had in using HyperCard. Next, we teachers paired the senior students with the grade 3 students. We were very conscious of positive partnerships, taking into consideration the students in both of our classes with learning problems, physical disabilities, developmental delays, and students for whom English was a second language.

One skill that we as teachers had to continually reinforce was the inclusion of the younger students. There was a tendency for the older students to take over in the computer room. This was not the case during the research component of the project, but when the students were using HyperCard, the older ones tended to make the decisions, leaving the younger students to observe the proceedings. As teachers, we monitored this situation by interacting with the students when they were working on the computer. We modeled appropriate ways of including the younger students and we discussed the issue with the older students, eliciting ways that they could teach the younger students some of the skills in HyperCard that they had learned. As our classes contained quite a number of students with special needs, we were able to get a teacher's assistant to work with our students. We specified that this assistant was to work with all the students rather than concentrating solely on the integrated students. Having the designation of special needs in no way guaranteed that this student would have challenges in inclusion. Often it was a nondesignated student or student pair that required support in collaboration. We also detailed strategies that we were using to help students include their partners in planning and constructing the HyperCard stack.

Even though we worked on these skills, some of the more-able learners had difficulty when working with students who did not grasp the skills required to use HyperCard. Both teachers spent more time with these groups modifying the task as required by limiting the number of cards needed, omitting animated sequences, and helping the students paraphrase the research materials. We also tried to diffuse these situations by allowing the more-able learners extra computer time to work independently on HyperCard projects pertinent to their studies in such other curriculum areas as Social Studies.

Evaluation

The excitement of participating in this buddy project was infectious in the extreme — for students of all ages! The idea for a Buddy Edition of our school newspaper came from a senior student. When it was published, this issue included numerous accounts by students in our classes of the HyperCard projects they were completing. A notable contribution was written by one of the younger students with a developmental delay, explaining how much he liked his two buddies.

My buddy's name is Erik.
He makes me laugh!
We made a hypercard stack together.
We are also writing a children's story.
Sometimes I push the wrong button on the computer, but Erik helps me.

Michael

My Buddies

My buddy is Scott.
We made gingerbread houses and we made a Hypercard stack.
The title is "Soccer".
Scott taught me how to make a button in Hypercard. Scott is very nice.

Hiroki

My two buddies are Alex and Ben. They helped out a lot. They taught me all about 'Sounds a Plenty'. Sounds a Plenty is a device that you can play sounds on. My buddies are very nice.

Darren

After three months of working together to complete our HyperCard projects, we had an Open House in the computer lab to celebrate our achievement. Parents, teachers, and students were invited to experience the HyperCard stacks. The designers of each stack explained to each guest how to navigate through the project. To make sure the older students continued to include the younger students during the explanations, we had coached them on ways to assist their younger partner in answering questions and demonstrating how the stack worked.

At the end of the Open House, the students completed self-evaluations of their HyperCard projects, which included information about the development of their HyperCard skills, their research skills, and their collaborative skills.

HYPERCARD SELF-EVALUATION

View your finished Hypercard stack to evaluate your work for the following:

Name Catherine   Partner's Name Liz

Originality 5/5
- ideas were original not a copy of someone else's

Clarity 4●/5
-the stack had a clear beginning, middle and end
-the story was clearly told so that the audience could follow it

Illustrations 4/5
-all illustrations that were used
will help the audience to understand the stack

Audio 5/5
-sounds or music were appropriate for the stack
-the sound was easily understood

Title card 5/5
-author's names were included
-title was clear
-graphics and illustrations were eye-catching

Overall Impact of the stack 4/5
-includes all of the above sections
-neatness

Cooperative behaviour 5/5
-my partner and I worked well together
-when we disagreed we talked until we reached a consensus

30/35

TOTAL 32/35

Comments:
Something I'd like you to notice about the stack is that it is only
for ages 10 and up

Since completing this project, my Hypercard skills have improved in the following areas in using icons and linking cards.

A problem that we had to overcome to complete this stack was ~~~~ to ask
every gr. 6 and gr. 7 student in the school during ressess
and lunch period
The grade that I feel this project should get is B-A because my partner
and I worked hard and spent a long time doing.

These evaluations provided valuable information to assist us in planning future lessons focusing on the inclusion of others. The ability to work cooperatively with others is a skill that the Business Association of Canada has identified as necessary for individuals in the workplace. Teaching these skills is a component of the Personal Planning curriculum. It is interesting to note that the students' self-evaluations are generally very accurate in reflecting the work that was done. In addition to their self-evaluation, the students were also expected to lead the teachers through the HyperCard stack in order to explain the positive and challenging aspects of their work.

The HyperCard project was successful in that it not only developed research and computer skills but it also developed the students' ability to solve problems and to collaborate. For many of the students, they now had a new friend in the school who was not in their grade. In terms of playground politics, this was been beneficial for a number of students. For the students with limited English this was a real bonus, because they have had the opportunity to get to know another student over a period of time. In several of these partnerships, a real bond was established between the students. The primary students now were able to create their own HyperCard stacks, and the intermediate students had developed skills in computer programming, a foundation for learning more complex computer skills at the secondary school level.

Updating Social Studies Projects

During a unit of study in Social Studies, students enjoy the opportunity to further explore topics introduced in class. Ancient Egypt continues to be a topic of particular interest to students in the upper intermediate grades. The unit encompasses such subtopics as mythology, geography, the Nile River, women in ancient Egypt, religious beliefs, agriculture, government, technological developments, written language, art and architecture, and structure of the society.

The accomplishments of the ancient Egyptians continue to fascinate. Each year, there are new archeological findings and theories that enable the study of ancient Egypt to be continually modified as new discoveries and scientific interpretations are made. This encourages an investigation of the media for the latest information on ancient Egypt. Recently, we included a discussion of modern Egypt after reading the media account of the murders of foreign tourists who were visiting the ancient temple of Hatshepsut, a female pharaoh of the New Kingdom period. This link to media helps students see hypotheses about ancient groups of people as not written in stone and therefore static but rather as bits of information to be considered in building an understanding of these ancient people.

About midway through the approximately two-month unit of study, the students are asked to think of two or three subtopics that have interested them about the ancient Egyptians. They then write down these topics and circulate among their peers to determine shared topics of interest and, for many, new topics of interest. After allowing sufficient time to elapse so that most students have discussed topics with at least one-third of the class, students find a classmate with whom they have a common topic of interest. Each pair or group of three (less desirable but needed in classes without an even number of students) must then report their proposed topic before beginning their research.

This is the initial stages of a HyperCard research project. Since the students generally have some knowledge of their topic, they sketch what their HyperCard Stack might look like, as a series of cards containing text, graphics, sound, and animation. This initial planning stage really helps to motivate the students, since at this point they can begin to envision the special effects they will employ to capture the attention of their audience. Once this rough plan is in place, the students are ready to begin research on their topic.

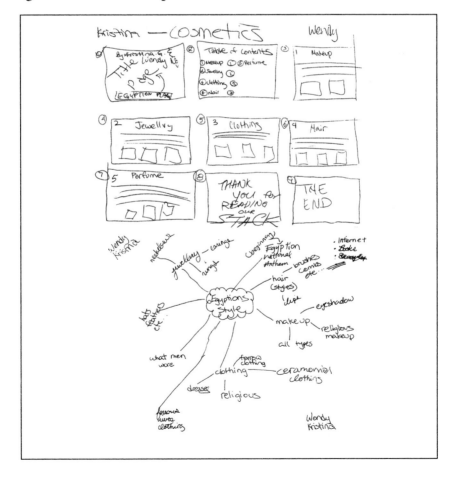

Using the Internet

We want the students to use the Internet as part of their research. To assist them in learning how to efficiently "surf the Net," we practise with several Net Search activities. Some of these we design, others the students design.

A Teacher-Designed Internet Search

INTERNET SEARCH

Buddies' names: Date:

From the Yahooligan's main menu, choose "Around the World."

1. What is the price of broccoli in today's stock market?

After you and your buddy have found the answer, leap over to Science and Oddities.

2. With what is Eddy the Eco-Dog armed?

Now that you are surfin' along, let's go to Orca Bay.

3. What happened to the Canucks on July 22, 1996?

4. 'Bear' with me, but what is the secondary logo of the Grizzlies that was presented to the team from the Chinook Indian band, and what does it mean?

5. Now, while you two do the Voodoo, find out what position Brent Thurston plays.

6. By the way, who is Danielle Dube?

Back to the Yahooligan's main menu. It's time for a snack and I'd like some Soup.

7. For all you artists, what is the name of the 'alternative' band from Ontario?

Wow, that was a lot of moving around. Now let's go directly to the URL: http://netpresence.com/npcgi/ttt

8. What do you get? Play a round.

On a cruise around the world let's go to the URL: http://www.sci.mus.mn.us/sln/ma/map.html

9. What is the name of the Bay?

A Student-Designed Internet Search

<u>Internet Search</u>

From the Yahooligans main menu go to movies under entertainment. Then go down to Walt Disney Pictures. Click on Disney. Go down and click on Pooh.

1) What is Pooh doing?
    Go home.
    Go to around the world. Then go to mythology and folklore. Go to animals, myths, and legends.

2) How many toes does Agor have?
    Go home.
    Go up to bookmarks, Yahoo. Go to games. Click on puzzles. Click on tic-tac-toe. Click on Christmas tic-tac-toe.

3) What are the X's?
    Go home.
    Go to movies under entertainment. Then go to Walt Disney Pictures.

4) What are the O's in Mr. Magoo doing?
    Go home.
    Go to space under science and oddities. Click on Mir Space Station.

5) What is Mir? Clue: Read the paragraphs to find out.
    Go home.
    Go to bookmarks, Yahoo. Environment under society and culture. Click on rivers, oceans, and other water. Click on waterfalls then on waterfalls page.

6) How many pictures of waterfalls are there?
    Go home.
    Go to web celeb under entertainment.

7) What is the address that you use if you want to write to the Green Bay Packers?
    Go home.
Click on sports and recreation. Click on snow sports. Click on winter sports foundation. Go down under sports and click on snowboarding. Go down and click on freestyle.

8) What colour is Kirsten Brown's hair?

By: Claire and Karlie

Students with Internet experience help their partners learn to navigate through this warm-up activity. We then teach a short lesson highlighting the functions of the software used by our computers to access the Internet (Netscape Communicator™ or Microsoft™ Internet Explorer). We have found ideas for lessons such as this in the user- friendly *Teacher's Complete and Easy Guide to the Internet* (Heide, Ann and Linda Stilbourne. Trifolium Books, 1996). Through exploration, the students will learn the use of bookmarks, Uniform Resource Locators (URLs), and search engines.

Keyword Searches

After these initial activities, students are ready to organize their topic into subtopics they can use in keyword searches. Using the Yahoo Canada search engine (www.yahoo.ca) to research the phrase "Ancient Egypt" yields many Web sites, a number of which are unrelated to the particular subtopic of interest to the student. The same search for "Ancient Egypt" using other search engines such as Infoseek (www.infoseek.com) or Excite (www.excite.com) yields other related Web sites, all of which are not useful to the students. The most difficult aspect of teaching students how to use the Internet is to enable them to choose the Web sites that provide useful information while avoiding time wasted investigating sites that do not contain relevant facts. Since the World Wide Web is not an organized source of information, the time factor becomes a central issue in using the Internet for research.

One strategy to assist students in finding useful Web sites is to provide a list of URLs (Uniform Resource Locators — Web site addresses). Sites in the World Wide Web usually begin with *www*. The teacher can preview the Web sites to determine those that are relevant to the topic. Students are then encouraged to add to the teacher's list any helpful URLs they have discovered. Thus, in a collaborative way, we are all engaged in finding and sharing information. Since Web sites are constantly being developed and others are taken off the Internet, URLs may be deleted at any time or the address may simply change. One good Web site containing information about Ancient Egypt was deleted six months later. This trend necessitates constant monitoring by anyone using the Internet.

When students locate information pertinent to their topic, they either record what they have read by paraphrasing the information in a set of conventional notes or they highlight the relevant portions of the text and save it on a floppy disk. This is a useful technique since the information can be imported into a word-processing program and the student then paraphrases it, selecting the relevant ideas to word process into paragraph format. Some students like this technique, as it negates note taking, yet others prefer the process of note taking because it gives them an organizational framework. Teachers need to be aware that some students will be inclined to plagiarize information if they are not systematically taught how to paraphrase what they read.

Photographs can also be selected from the Internet and be imported as graphics into a HyperCard stack.

One interesting trend since introducing the use of the Internet for research purposes is that students do not seem to maintain the interest in sifting through the Web sites that are related to their research project. A growing number of students decide that they would rather use books and other printed material for the majority of their research rather than devote the time needed to locate relevant information from Web sites.

Organizing the Information

The information gathered is then organized into a HyperCard stack as a series of cards that explain the topic of study to the audience. Students are taught how to add sounds, animation, and special effects to make their project more interesting. We also discuss and experiment with such design considerations as balancing text and graphics with the need to convey information about the topic. With more practice in completing these kinds of research projects, the HyperCard stacks that the students produce improve.

The collaborative nature of working on the computer results in students who are teaching each other the finer points of computer programming using HyperText. Often students who had learned a new script, a HyperText computer command, teach it to a group of interested students in a mini-lesson. The script is then recorded on the board for reference and students often incorporate these into their stacks. Notice the variety in the samples from the following students, all working on the topic of Ancient Egypt.

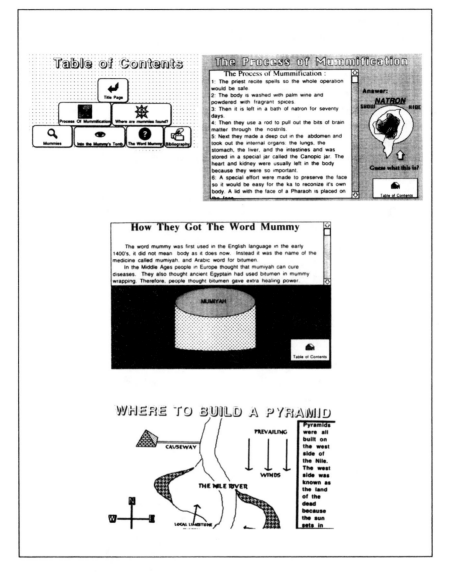

HyperCard Evaluation

A HyperCard project is written to be viewed by an audience. Students need to receive feedback about their accomplishments. Therefore, we usually have an Open House for students and interested parents to see the projects. This is a very useful process since some of the students encounter new HyperCard users who are unfamiliar with navigating through a HyperCard stack. Stacks that are poorly organized or contain information not clearly written tend to confuse their audience. The chance to see how others access the information in their stacks often provides students with good insights as to how they will improve their work in future projects.

Prior to showing the stack to the teacher, an evaluation sheet is given to each pair of students who completed the activity. The students complete their self-evaluation; then, together, we read their evaluation and view the stack. The students' job is to lead the teacher through the cards. At the end of the viewing, we go through each section of the evaluation and the teacher adds her evaluation. Generally, the students tend to be very critical of themselves. The teacher's view provides a balance of the overall product. Here are two different formats for evaluation that we have used.

HYPERCARD EVALUATION

Name:_____

STUDENT'S MARK   TEACHER'S MARK

View your completed HyperCard Stack to evaluate your work for the following:

Title Card   /5   /5

- title was clear and eyecatching
- information was organized so that the audience would quickly understand the topic of your project
- the author's name was displayed

Audio   /5   /5
(may or may not be present)

- sounds, voice, or music were appropriate for the stack and added to the overall effect
- sound quality was clear

Clarity   /5   /5

- the cards in the stack were linked together in a way that would make sense to an audience
- all information was clear and thorough, which allowed the audience to learn about your topic

Special Effects   /5   /5
and Scripts

- a variety of effects and scripts were used to add interest to your stack
- your audience could easily follow your stack without difficulty
- all buttons were linked to the next card in an organized way

Text   /5   /5

- conventions of writing such as spelling, capitalization, punctuation and paragraphing were followed. If any of these errors exist, they will not distract the reader.

Overall Impact   /5   /5
of the Stack

- the stack is complete
- all aspects of the stack work together to communicate what I know
  about my topic
- my work is neatly and clearly laid out on each card

TOTAL   /   /

INFORMATION AND QUESTIONS FOR MY AUDIENCE

I would like you to notice that in this HyperCard Stack

_____

_____

In this HyperCard stack I learned more about my topic, especially

_____

_____

A HyperCard script is computer programming using HyperText computer
language. One of the scripts which I have used in this stack allowed me to

_____

_____

A problem that I had to overcome in this stack was

_____

_____

What did your audience particularly enjoy about the HyperCard stack?

_____

_____

Other comments from your audience

_____

_____

HYPERCARD PROJECT
EVALUATION

PROJECT TITLE: _Using To do and What voda_ NAME OF CREATOR(s) Matt
(handwritten above: When did Prehistoric People start they?)
Jason

Please notice that this stack _very detailed drawings_

My skills in HyperCard have improved in the following areas: _Making fields and_
using the pencil tool to draw better drawings. Also different
fonts and effects with the pencil.
A new skill that I have learned as a result of completing this project is: _How to_
flip writing and turn the writing into interesting shapes

One surprising fact that I learned through research on the topic is: _How hard it_
must have been to make these tools.

While working with a partner I learned that _When working equally, the project_
goes much faster

Additional comments: _This was one of my better Hypercard projects._

Rate yourself on the following components of the stack:

1. Title page - (eyecatching, includes a title and names of the creators, special effects add
to the level of interest)   5/5 student   5/5 teacher

2. Information - (were the facts arranged in an interesting way? Will the reader learn
about the topic by exploring the stack? Were all of the subtopics related to the overall topic
of the stack?)   14/15   14/15

3. Special effects - (did I include special effects that added to any stack or did the effects
confuse my audience? Was I able to include a Hide and Show button that worked? If I used
sound or animation were the results clear?)
       8/10   8/10

4. overall impact of the stack - (was your project clear, interesting, and accurate? Did you
include enough information about the topic in the stack?)
       18/20   19/20

Total   45/50   46/50

Information is clearly displayed & repeated to help the audience-

| | Special Facts | |

Neandertals were the first people to bury there dead. They layed flowers on their dead relatives in their graves. Did you know that Neandertals had almost the same amount of injuries as rodeo riders. They had more head injuries than any other injury to their bodies.

(Bar chart, %, scale 0 to 40 in increments of 10)
Categories: Foot, Leg, Pelvis, Hand, Arm, Trunk, Head
Legend: ■ Neandertals   ▨ Rodeo Riders

10 Mathematics

Fostering Mathematical Thinking

The basics of mathematics are expanding. No longer is math simply number sense. The *Curriculum and Evaluation Standards for School Mathematics* (National Council of Teachers of Mathematics. Reston, VA: The Council, 1989) suggest four unifying themes in the teaching of mathematics: mathematics as problem solving, mathematics as communication, mathematical reasoning, and mathematical connections.

In our classroom, we wanted the students to become good problem solvers, both with numbers and with manipulative materials. Using manipulatives would provide a good starting point to increase students' ease in using the language of mathematics. These materials would keep mathematics activity based rather than based on exercises using memory, formula, or abstract language that many of the students associated with mathematics.

We also wanted to encourage students to reflect on their learning in mathematics. Writing could be embedded in mathematics assignments. Students could record their thinking in mathematics journals, and then look back and notice their development. We hoped that students would start to question whether or not they had all the information they needed to reach a decision, not just quickly jump to conclusions. We wanted to nurture a world of mathematical thinkers. The students' writing in the mathematics journals would enable we teachers to view the conclusions they were drawing. Armed with this information, we could provide more opportunities or more conversation to help students match their thinking and reasoning with their results. As students reached for language that matched their thinking, they would increase their ability to communicate mathematically.

We wanted our students to work in heterogeneous mathematics teams. Working together would enable them to build on one another's thinking, to clarify their own thinking, and hopefully to learn that there is more than one right way in mathematics.

Finally, we wanted all our students to believe in themselves as mathematicians as they experienced success working with materials and understanding what they were doing. We wanted students to develop confidence in themselves as mathematical thinkers, to celebrate their successes, large and small.

The last area of our curriculum to change was mathematics. Feeling rather insecure, we turned for support to Linda Beatty, Curriculum Coordinator for Mathematics in the Delta, B.C., School Division. With her guidance, we began our change. Gone were silent mathematics classrooms where some students searched for right answers and others waited anxiously for the bell to ring. Moving in were more thoughtful experiences with mathematics that enabled all students to move along a continuum of development and individually and collectively become more successful.

Tangrams — Getting Started

We chose to work on developing spatial reasoning using tangrams. To set the stage and invite curiosity, a week before the actual unit began we introduced a puzzle. The goal of the puzzle was to determine what the new manipulative material would be. Each day, we gave the students a clue to this puzzle and invited their best guess. A grid with the students' names was posted. Any attempt was recorded. If and when a student guessed the correct material, a happy face was placed next to her or his name and the student was sworn to secrecy. The clues, given one per day, were as follows:

Day 1 — There is a legend surrounding this material.

Day 2 — This material has three different shapes.

Day 3 — Five of the pieces are the same shape but different sizes.

Day 4 — There are two congruent pairs in this set.

Day 5 — There is one square and one parallelogram and five triangles.

Tangrams — Developing Spatial Reasoning

As the week progressed, students began to correctly guess what the new material would be. There was a constant buzz as they examined and re-examined the clues, coaching each other and trying to describe their connections without giving away the answer.

On the last day of the week, we talked about spatial sense and what it meant in our lives. Some of the ideas the students explored were:

- jigsaw puzzles
- tiling a floor
- estimating distance when driving
- setting a table
- designing a house
- playing pool
- playing Nintendo™

On the following Monday, students were told the Chinese legend surrounding the tangrams. The tangram puzzle is said to have originated in China hundreds of years ago. One of the stories often told suggests that a Chinese man had a beautiful ceramic tile he had made. One day, he dropped it and it broke into seven pieces. It took him a long time to put it back together. The first Chinese book to contain tangram puzzles was written in the early 1800s. Tangrams themselves were considered to already be very old at that time.

Students were then given a package of plastic tangrams each and encouraged to explore them. Once this was complete, we added the layer of mathematical language, talking about:

- congruence (with pairs of triangles)
- square (made of two small triangles)
- parallel lines (on the parallelogram and the square)
- symmetry (1 line, 2 lines, or many lines)
- angles (right, obtuse, and acute)

Students were required to demonstrate what they could build, first as a team, then as individuals. With 3 triangles (2 small, 1 mid-sized), 5 triangles, and 7 pieces, they built:

1. square
2. rectangle
3. triangle
4. parallelogram
5. trapezoid

We made a wall chart, as follows, and encouraged students to fill their name in on the chart as they solved one of the puzzles. This not only made the learning visible and was extremely motivating but also gave the students a reason to stand up and move from their desks — an experience often discouraged, but definitely beneficial in helping students maintain attention.

	3 pieces	5 pieces	7 pieces
square			
rectangle			
triangle			
parallelogram			
trapezoid			

Once the team had built all these shapes, each student pair received a tangram card and individually they demonstrated how to build each shape. These cards were checked by the teacher, then traded in as each shape was completed. The conversations and thinking were really evident during this exercise as the cards were distributed randomly, so the degree of difficulty of each puzzle was unpredictable. To monitor how many puzzles had been completed, each pair of students was given a Post-it note to attach to the top of their working space. They wrote their names on this Post-it, and then tallied the number of cards they had completed. These tally sheets could then be transferred directly to our record-keeping book, to keep track of the students' practice sessions.

Prepared tangram puzzle cards are available from many different sources. We have used *Tangramables* (Martschinke, Judi. Deerfield, IL: Learning Resources, 1990) and *The Puzzling World of Tangrams and Pentominoes* (Jones, Grant. Barrie, ON: Exclusive Educational Products, 1998).

Following this practice, the students each receive booklets to complete. These booklets require them to build a tangram on top, and then build the tangrams using slides (move off the outline), flips (mirror image), and turns (90 degrees). The students found these books much easier to complete, even though they were now working individually. The booklets progressed in difficulty, moving from puzzles requiring three pieces, to five pieces to seven pieces.

Finally, each student was asked to build a tangram puzzle that could be included in a booklet for a younger buddy class. This was an important aspect of the lesson sequence, because it enabled students to work creatively in mathematics.

Writing was an integral part of these lessons. At the end of each new segment, the students wrote to record their mathematical accomplishments and their mathematical thinking. Thus they had six opportunities to write:

1. after free exploration
2. after making shapes
3. after working with the cards
4. after tangram booklets, not using slides, flips and turns
5. after completing slides, flips and turns
6. after making their own shape.

Notice the reflections of Rachel and Nicole. They demonstrate the inclusion of students and the students' growth in understanding and pride in their accomplishments.

Evaluation — Collecting Performance Data

We built in a performance assessment for this unit. Students sat in tables of four. We gave the students a tangram card, then asked them, individually, to demonstrate a slide, a flip, and a turn. They exchanged cards as we requested each new demonstration. Collecting performance data was easy in this setting. We used the chart on page 137 to collect information on their learning.

Rachel

① Free Exploration
In the time I had to make things
out of the shapes I made quite a few
things I made 2 different sized
squares, a christmas tree, a rectangle, a dog,
and a parallelogram with half a triangle
stiching out.

② Making Shapes
I felt frustrated but happy. I
could make 6 shapes out of 15. I didn't
get a chance to try a few of them.

③ Working with Cards
I found it easy to work with shapes and fit them
into the right spot. Most were easy but some
were challenging.

④ Tangram Booklets
What fits here??!! I Got it!
I can't understand! Yes! Starts
easy, gets hard then easier.
Some shapes were hard but
mostly easy. Sometimes a
remaining peice was too big
for the last place. There
was only one of those!
That was the hard one.

⑤ Slides Flips and Turns
Making the slide was easy
because you only have to look at
the picture and copy it After.
Flip's the rectocoordes easy
Upside down flips are probably
easy also. Turns are also
easy.

⑥ My book
Making a shape was
easy because I got
the Idea from Janice
who sits beside me
Almost everything
was easy! Math is easy

Avery's cardy dog

Nicole

1. Free Exploration
I made a house.

2. Making shapes
It was easy!

3. Working with cards.
too easy! I liked it!

4. Tangram Booklets
I see pictures in my head.

MY book
a dancer

Tangram Assessment

Name: _____ Date: _____

CONCEPTS	Confident	Meets Expectations	Needs Support
1. Completes tasks successfully. 2. Discusses mathematical connections: flips, slides, turns symmetry congruency angles 3. Explains experiences in journal.			
WORK HABITS			
1. Perseveres to complete task. 2. Takes risks (willing to try). 3. Uses a variety of strategies. 4. Asks questions related to task. 5. Creates new puzzles/problems. 6. Does good self-evaluation.			
SMALL-WORK GROUP			
1. Cooperates with peers. 2. Demonstrates leadership skills. 3. Listens well. 4. Supports group members/partners.			

Adapted from: *World's Most Popular Puzzles and Problems Pentominoes* (Jones, Grant. Barrie, ON: Exclusive Educational Products, 1996).

11 Teaching a Class Novel

The Need to Study a Whole Class Novel

There are times in a combined or multiage class when the students in one grade are studying one novel while, simultaneously, the students in the other grade are studying a different novel. This experience is not always positive. It can be organizationally challenging for the teacher and may leave us feeling less than effective. Nonetheless, from time to time, most teachers feel the need for each grade to study a whole class novel. At these times, we focus on investigation of the writer's craft and a subsequent critical analysis. This requires that all participants have read the same novel and can enter into a conversation about it. We also use this time to examine particular authors or genres, and to teach specific vocabulary, sentence structure, and literary elements.

We began our study by turning to the *B.C. Curriculum Guide for Language Arts* and choosing our Learning Outcomes:

Comprehend and Respond (Comprehension)   gr. 6

- identify and represent the main ideas or events in stories
- use information they have read, heard, or viewed to develop questions and activities that will extend their understanding
- organize details and information they have read, heard, or viewed using a variety of written and graphic forms, including charts, webs, and maps

- locate and interpret details to answer specific questions or complete task

Comprehend and Respond (Engagement and Personal Response)   **gr. 6**

- compare real and imaginary times and places portrayed in literature with their own time and place

Comprehend and Respond (Comprehension)   **gr. 7**

- demonstrate understanding of the main ideas or events in novels
- use information they have read, heard, or viewed in a variety of written or graphic forms, including written notes and charts
- locate and interpret details in print to gather information and build understanding
- identify point of view in literary communications
- describe and locate examples of literary elements, including plot, climax, resolution, conflict, theme, and setting

Comprehend and Respond (Engagement and Personal Response)   **gr. 7**

- make explicit connections between themes, characters, and events in literature and their own experiences or other literature

We determined that such aspects of the novel as plot development and characterization would be dealt with separately. However, both groups needed to be able to use this information, with supporting details, in different forms. The grade 7s were required to describe and locate more literary elements. We decided to teach literary elements such as setting, character, plot, and theme to both groups, with references made to both novels. The novels would be chosen from the Ministry of Education's list of recommended resources.

The Plan — Setting Up the Grade Groups

We chose to address student learning in the spring term by using the allotted resource time to jointly teach the two novel study groups. In this way, we could still target the students who were less-developed readers but we could do this in the context of the class learning goals. We also wanted to involve these students in discussion groups with more-able readers to model and encourage meaningful connections and thoughtful conversations. Our timetable for this included two consecutive forty-minute periods as well as one other forty-minute period each week. The grade 6 novel we chose was *The True Confessions of Charlotte Doyle* by Avi. The grade 7 novel was *Log Jam* by Monica Hughes. We chose these novels because both involved main characters whose personalities develop through their experiences in the novel and, thematically, both novels investigate the concept of justice. As well, we felt both novels to be worthy of the time and to be novels the students were not reading on their own.

Once the students received their novels, they met in grade groups. From time to time, we moved to separate places in the school, for ease of communication.

On the first day, the two groups explored their new novels by predicting the plot based on the book jackets, book blurbs, illustrations, and on prior knowledge of the author. Several grade 7 students had read novels by Monica Hughes, so they were keen to share their knowledge of her science-fiction writing.

The Process — Reflection Journals and Discussion

We expected students to read much of their novel independently, but also allowed some time in each session for silent reading. At this time, we teachers had conversations with individual students, to help monitor their comprehension and to gain insights into their understanding.

As the novel study progressed, we required that each student keep a journal of reflections about the novel. Notice these samples. Don, one of the students with a severe learning disability, generates a series of plot-related questions in an attempt to respond to the novel. Anna, on the other hand, is a very able reader and easily responds in a more personal way, weaving together her experiences and thoughts with those of the author.

When students were having problems understanding the events in the plot due to reading problems or language difficulties, the discussion raised by others could help clarify their difficulty. For example, Don was confused by the chronology of events in *The True Confessions of Charlotte Doyle*. The students in the group discussed the main events in

Pg #	Chapter	thought
7	1	Why is she going to America?
10	1	What is the problem with Captain Jaggery?
11	1	Where is Captain Jaggery?
13	1	Why does Avi dragg Zonandon?
19	2	What significans is the coach?
24	2	Why does he stare at her?
30	3	Captain Jaggery seems cery.
31	3	Who is this Cranick "Profit?"
31	3	
32	3	This seems to exaderated. (hiswhg)
33	3	Jaggery is to nice.
34	3	Why does she cry? (she duess it)
		Don

Anna

I wondered why both the porters dropped her trunk and ran when they heard the name Captain Jaggery or Sea hawk. Why was the second mate, Mr. keetch trying to stop her from sailing with them? I think that the Seahawk is going to turn out to be a pirate ship. If I was Charlotte Doyle I would probably run away back to the Barrington School for Better Girls instead of sailing on the Seahawk. Zacharia might have given her the knife because he thought someone was going to kill her. Or maybe he was about to kill her himself and used it as a cover-up. The author would have had some experiance, probably on ships to be able to... write in such detail. I would've thought that Charlotte would act more drasticly when she heard the Captain and second mate talking about keeping the other people off and using her as a wittness.

the plot, then created pie charts in their reflective journals, including both illustrations and phrases to describe the events. Not only was Don able to use this information to better understand the novel, but all students were directed toward two specific learning outcomes:

- *locate and interpret details to answer specific questions of complete tasks*
- *describe information provided in simple and direct illustrations, maps, charts, or other graphic representations*

Notice the different pie charts created by Don and Anna.

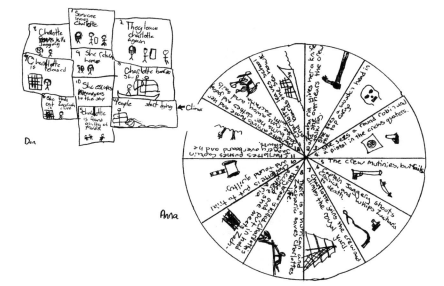

Don

Anna

The study of character development focused on changes the students noted in the character throughout the novel. The grade 6 students came up with the idea that the main character's actions in the beginning of the novel were dictated by her naiveté, but they noted that she gained experience through the novel and this, in turn, influenced her actions. One of the students' use of the word *naive* prompted other members of the group to consult a dictionary to confirm that this was an appropriate way to describe the character. At this moment, we realized that the students had taken ownership of the literature group and that their realizations would shape the direction of the discussion. They had indeed internalized the questioning mind of the literature circles upon which we had previously worked.

Since characterization was a major learning outcome for this novel study, we followed the student's lead and we examined Charlotte through the lens of naive behavior. The students then worked in small groups to find evidence to support the idea that she behaved in naive ways and that she was gaining experience towards the end of the novel. Students recorded their findings with page references in a chart and compared their evidence with the rest of the group.

The grade 7 group looked at how the main character's aboriginal heritage could have influenced the course of events in the novel. These students group also looked for evidence in the novel to support their positions.

Discussion in the literature groups for both grade levels then moved from character development to theme. The concept of justice was discussed. Had the main characters been treated fairly by the legal system? The debates in both groups were so lively, we turned to a **Mock Trial**. The students had previously participated in class debates and in Hot Seat activities, so their background knowledge was quite developed.

Each of the students then chose a role. The volunteers for the positions of defense lawyer and prosecutor had large speaking roles, and we encouraged students to volunteer for these roles if they either had well-developed oral communication skills *or* if they wished to practise to enhance these skills.

Together we sculpted the wording of the charges. The grade 7 trial focused on whether or not Isaac had been fairly treated by the legal system. The grade 6 trial focused on Charlotte's innocence. During the month-long preparation for the trial, students worked in small groups to record evidence in the form of direct quotes from the text to use either in support of, or against, the character. The students were also asked to anticipate and record the questions that might be asked in court by the lawyers and prosecutors. The "plus" evidence and questions were in defense of Charlotte, the "minus" were the prosecution's case.

The majority of students participated in the mock trial as witnesses, which required that they understand their character well enough to be able to answer questions. This was a new process for them and they needed a lot of assistance and rehearsal to gather evidence and to use it in role.

All the anticipated questions were collected and given to the respective lawyers for consideration. Depending on the questioning strategy, these questions could be used by either the defense or the prosecution in preparing their cases. At this point, we teachers assumed the roles of defense lawyer and prosecutor to role-play possible strategies for questioning the defendants and witnesses. After we had asked several questions, we would have the class explain the thinking behind our line of questioning. Making the thinking explicit was critical to the students' mastery of this form of questioning. To assist the lawyers and prosecutors in developing a questioning strategy, we held conferences to discuss the case. Such choices as who they would want to question as character witnesses and what physical evidence they might need were

Carrie

Topic - Charges
Was Charlotte Doyle unfairly tried?   Role: Keetch

PAGE	PLUS	MINUS	PLUS QUESTIONS	MINUS QUESTIONS
200	Keetch told the captain everything that happened on the ship.	Keetch was going to get an innocent person killed by telling the captain she was coming.	How did the captain know she was coming?	What was the consequence of Keetch telling the captain she was coming?
95, 96	"I'll give you the privilege to choose one." ... "I don't want to".	To choose one to get punished.	What did the captain tell Charlotte.	What did the captain ask Charlotte to choose?
153, 154	"Hollybrass his murder" ... "What's that got to do with not calling me?" ... "The Captain" ... "It was you."	Because she did not know why she was not called.	How come she was not called?	Why did Keetch's face have a look of fear on it?
194	"But who did it then?" ... "Captain Jaggery." ...	He was the only one beside Zacharia that knew where the knife was.	Who murdered Hollybrass?	Did the captain know where the knife was?
17	I warned Charlotte to take another ship.	Mr. Grummage insisted that this was a fine ship, and she was not to take another.	What did you warn Charlotte?	Why did Charlotte not take another ship?

discussed during these conferences. The students returned again and again to their novels, searching for specific evidence to support their cases.

Setting Evaluation Criteria for Mock Trials

To set the criteria for evaluation of the mock trials, we asked the students, as a whole class, to describe the characteristics of a good presentation for this assignment. All of their ideas were noted, and then grouped as a series of criteria statements.

Criteria for Individuals Participating in the Mock Trial
- staying in character (court personnel, characters from the novel)
- audible and clear voice
- questions and responses had to make sense with the novel
- appropriate body language

We found that the students did not independently include "explicit text references or details which indicated comprehension." We explained why we valued this criterion statement, then added it to our list. As a rule of thumb, we limit the list of criteria for evaluation to four or five to enable students to focus on the development of these skills.

Criteria for Individuals Participating in the Mock Trial
- staying in character (court personnel, characters from the novel)
- audible and clear voice
- questions and responses had to make sense with the novel
- appropriate body language
- explicit text reference or details which indicate comprehension

---

As teachers, we generated a performance scale to use in conjunction with the criteria. We gave this to the students and discussed it with them prior to the evaluation. As well, the students used both the criteria and the performance scale to evaluate both of us during our questioning of various witnesses. This allowed them to begin to internalize the criteria for success in a guided practice situation. They gave us feedback using these scales, and helped us set goals for future performances.

During the student presentations, we noted that most of the students seemed quite comfortable in their roles and we attributed this to the fact that they have watched countless hours of television court scenes. Even the ESL students were quite fluent in specialized vocabulary! Next time we do a similar unit, we will include a fieldtrip to a courtroom to watch the proceedings. Another pretrial activity would be to plan a viewing and subsequent discussion of a television trial. The ability to think about their roles before they actually had to act them out would allow the students to respond in more thoughtful ways.

Students had our criterion list and performance scale for their personal evaluation. We also scored the performances, and gave our results to the students. The students highlighted the criteria they wished to enhance, and then we repeated the trials, using different defense lawyers and prosecutors. This time, the student received feedback only on the criteria that he or she had highlighted as goal areas. Some students even came for additional coaching on their targeted goal area. We were extremely pleased with the students' participation, understanding of the novel, and ability to internalize the life of a specific character.

Reflections

We have come to really understand the power of building criteria with students (Gregory, Kathleen, Caren Cameron and Anne Davies. *Setting and Using Criteria*. Merville, BC: Connections Press, 1997). Continuing with the theme of justice, we read *Underground to Canada* by Barbara Smucker and *Freedom Train* by Dorothy Sterling. This time, we did not divide the students by grade. Instead, we explained that the former novel was a more challenging read and let the students choose. We were not completely satisfied with the quality of responses we had seen, in general, from the students in the study of *The True Confessions of Charlotte Doyle* and *Log Jam*. Certainly, as evidenced by Anna's response, there were some students who were responding in a sophisticated manner. However, the majority required more scaffolding. We provided the students with a list of criteria to aim toward when writing their chapter responses. As we read through the novel, we continually referred to these criteria and directly coached the students on how best to incorporate these into their responses. When the response journals were collected for our feedback, we teachers tailored our responses directly to the criteria. As a class, we decided that achieving five of these criteria in a thoughtful manner would constitute a powerful response, three or four could be competent, and less than that was developing.

Criteria for Powerful Journal Responses
- illustrations with captions
- predictions: "What do you think will happen?"
- words I don't know and my predictions for these words based on the rest of the sentence
- questions such as "I wonder why…"
- plot summary — in words, charts, point form, or mind map
- conversation with the author, "I like it when you…", "I wondered why you…"
- emotional response

The following responses represent three very different students:

Jezy is ESL and has been in Canada for just four months, Amy is a less-able reader, while Jagpur is an avid, able reader. Notice the depth of response from all three students. All the students were more able to respond deeply when guided by the criteria. As teachers, we ensure that our students really understand the explicit expectations of our tasks.

'peck of trouble'
Jezy

Freedom Train

predictions - Harriet went to the other work place,
   Ms Sarah sold her.

words - covered, creaked, sunup.

plot - After Harriet went out, Ms Sarah went to find
   her, she told to her mom, she wanted to hide,
   she don't want went back to that house again,
   but she can't, so she continue to thought or looked
   the window! Then her father bring her back, but
   Ms Sarah don't wa. her to helped.

Question -- Harriet ran away. and her father couldn't

   help her, I think her father was very sad.
   - Harriet ran away, if Ms Sarah don't want her,
   Where could Harriet went?

Julilly —

— mammy Sally

Julilly and mammy are getting split up.

Amy

Pg. 18-21   Chapter #2   Oct. 21, 97

    My prediction was right they got split ~~sliped~~ up. (Julilly and Mammy Sally).

    This fat man, the slave trainer ~~trader~~ sounds very mean and greedy. Why did the author make Julilly and Mammy Sally get split up?

    When Julilly was on the cart and crying, I felt like crying. I like the way how the author touches you that way.

the Wagon Julilly was in

Jagpur

i crack!

Oct. 21, 1997   Chapter 1

Prediction: I think that Julily will try to escape next time they rest. ~~and I~~

what I liked {
I liked the way the authors described the slave trader. I also think the description of Julily's feelings was very good ~~itso~~

Questions {
I don't understand why the slave Trader only took the children and not many adults I think that! the adults would be more valuable cause they can do more work.

12 Piecing It Together: Reporting and Conferencing

Criterion-Referenced Assessment

No writing about today's grade 4 to 7 classrooms would be complete without a comment about reporting. In British Columbia, our mandate is to write structured written reports three times a year, focusing on what the student is able to do, what the student needs support with, and establishing goals for further learning. In the intermediate grades, these comments are tied to letter grades, which in turn are based on the student's achievement against prescribed learning outcomes. Some provinces tie their comments to percentage marks, while others do not require a letter grade or a percentage. All provinces and states, however, are moving toward prescribed learning outcomes or expectations.

Reporting becomes more manageable as we continue to refine our work with criterion-referenced assessment. Both students and teachers can more easily describe powerful performances based on criteria, and can more easily articulate what learning goals would be most effective, judging the performance against these explicit criteria. It may be that this explicitness will finally free teachers to move away from mandates and politics and truly focus on student-centered learning. When working with criteria tied to learning outcomes or expectations, there is no escaping fuzzy lessons or classrooms where nothing much seems to be happening.

This learning/evaluation focus enables students to more easily talk about their learning, because they have been ongoing participants in the conversation that creates the expectations and goals. As they develop these communication skills, their ability to reflect on their learning and their ability to describe their learning to others improve. This leads students then to three-way conferences.

Three-Way Conferences

Our three-way conference usually follows the report card, although some teachers generate their report cards at the three-way conference (Davies, A., C. Cameron, C. Politano, and K. Gregory. 1992. *Together Is Better: Collaborative Assessment, Evaluation and Reporting*. Winnipeg, MB: Peguis). The participants in the conference include the teacher, parents, and the student. The conference places more ownership on the student to describe her or his achievement and allows more time and focus on the student's work.

Generally, each conference takes about fifteen minutes, followed by a parent/student look at work that has been completed that term. The conference usually begins with the teacher asking the student to describe learning of which he or she is particularly proud and to describe his/her goals for the next term. During the conference, the students review their work in all subjects, noting their strengths and their goals for next term. The teacher attempts to mediate the conversation between the parent and the student, but not to lead it, as her voice has already been heard in the report card. Questions the parent poses are directed to the student first. If a problem arises, the teacher tries to ensure that all parties have a chance to contribute. Once the overview is complete, the student takes his/her parents to show and describe the term's work, with examples from each subject. The class has often made these choices before.

We have found this form of conferencing to be well received by all participants. It is an authentic way of reviewing growth in specific skills, in communication, and in student thinking over a term. It values the learner and models a learner-centered environment. It also demonstrates lifelong learning. Parents are amazed at their children's ability to articulate their accomplishments and their learning goals. Often this is the most sustained "learning" conversation they have had in some time!

All students can participate. With students whose parents are more comfortable in a language other than English, the language of the conference moves between the two languages, sometimes with a translator, sometimes with the student being the language link. Students with other special educational needs, too, are the key link in the communication process, describing their accomplishments and their goals, using the class's prescribed learning outcomes as well as their Individualized Education Plans. Parents can see how their sons and daughters are working toward grade-appropriate learning goals with differentiated support but they do not have to worry about a watered down curriculum.

Finally, as teachers, we can relish and learn from the conversations that happen within the families. We observe more and talk less. From these observations, we pick up the pieces and join them with the curriculum expectations for the design of the next term.

Related Reading

Professional Literature

Atwell, N. 1987. *In the Middle*. Portsmouth, NH: Heinemann.

Bingham, J. 1985. *Samuel Maclure, Architect*. Ganges, BC: Horsdal and Schubart.

British Columbia Ministry of Education, Skills and Training. 1996. *English Language Arts K to 7. Integrated Resource Package*. Victoria, BC.

British Columbia Ministry of Education and Ministry Responsible for Multiculturalism and Human Rights. 1994. *Evaluating Reading Across Curriculum: Using the Reading Reference Set to Support Learning and Enhance Communication*. Victoria, BC.

Brownlie, F. and J. King. In Press. *Inclusion: Possibilities and Practices*.

Brownlie, F. and S. Close. 1992. *Beyond Chalk and Talk*. Markham, ON: Pembroke.

Brownlie, F., S. Close and L. Wingren. 1990. *Tomorrow's Classroom Today*. Markham, ON: Pembroke.

_____. 1988. *Reaching for Higher Thought*. Edmonton, AB: Arnold.

Davies, A., C. Cameron, C. Politano, and K. Gregory. 1992. *Together Is Better. Collaborative Assessment, Evaluation and Reporting*. Winnipeg, MB: Peguis.

Fielding, L. and D. Pearson, "Reading Comprehension: What Works."
1994. *Educational Leadership*, Vol. 51, #5.

Fogarty, R. 1997. *Problem-Based Learning and Other Curriculum Model for the Multiple Intelligences Classroom*. Arlington Heights, Illinois.

_____. 1990. "People Search." Richmond, BC: Thoughtful Cooperative Learning Workshop.

Goodman, D. 1990. *The Complete HyperCard 2.0 Handbook*. New York: Random House.

Gregory, K., C. Cameron, and A. Davies. 1997. *Setting and Using Criteria*. Merville, BC: Connections Publishing.

Heide, A. and L. Stilbourne. 1996. *The Teacher's Complete and Easy Guide to the Internet*. Toronto, ON: Trifolium Books.

Jeroski, S., F. Brownlie and L. Kaser. 1990, 1991. *Reading and Responding, Evaluation Resources for Teachers* (grades 4, 5, and 6). Scarborough, ON: Nelson Canada.

LeMahieu, P. 1996. "Portfolio Assessment." Richmond, BC: Paper presented at *Assessing for Success*.

McGee, L. 1996. "Grand Conversations as Social Contexts for Literary Work." New York: Paper presented at the American Education Research Association Conference.

_____. 1991. *Thinking in the Classroom*, Vol. 2. Victoria, BC: Assessment, Evaluation, and Reporting Branch.

Noonan, R.J. and R.G. Craig. 1988. *Mock Trial 1 — Regina vs Brogue*. Victoria, BC: Legal Service Society of BC., Ministry of the Attorney General.

Short, K. 1990. "Creating a Community of Learners." *Talking About Books: Creating Literate Communities*. Portsmouth, NH: Heinemann.

Spandel, V. and R.J. Stiggens. 1990. *Creating Writers*. New York: Longman.

Wells, G. 1986. *The Meaning Makers. Children Learning Language and Using Language to Learn*. Portsmouth, NH: Heinemann.

Children's Literature

Avi. 1990. *The True Confessions of Charlotte Doyle*. New York: Avon Books.

Bailey, L. 1992. *How Come the Best Clues Are Always in the Garbage?* Toronto, ON: Kids Can Press.

Boraks-Nemetz, L. 1994. *The Old Brown Suitcase*. Brentwoord Bay, BC: Ben-Simon Publications.

Cherry, L. 1992. *The River Ran Wild*. New York: Harcourt Brace Jovanovich.

Choi, S.N. 1993. *Echoes of the White Giraffe*. New York: Bantam Doubleday Dell.

Choi, S.N. 1991. *Year of Impossible Goodbyes*. New York: Bantam Doubleday Dell.

Filipovic, Z. 1994. *Zlata's Diary*. New York: Penguin Books.

Frank, A. 1952. *The Diary of Anne Frank*. New York: Simon and Schuster.

Garrigue, S. 1985. *The Eternal Spring of Mr. Ito*. Don Mills, ON: Maxwell Macmillan.

Hughes M. 1987. *Log Jam*. Toronto: Irwin.

King, Jr., Dr. M.L. 1997. *I Have a Dream*. New York: Scholastic.

Kogawa, J. "Hiroshima Exit." 1989. In *Themes, on a Journey*, Barry James, ed. Scarborough, ON: Nelson.

Laird, E. 1991. *Kiss the Dust*. London: Mammoth.

Levitin, S. 1987. *The Return*. New York: Fawcett Juniper.

Lowry, L. 1989. *Number the Stars*. New York: Bantam.

Smucker, B. 1979. *Days of Terror*. Markham, ON: Penguin

Smucker, B. 1978. *Underground to Canada*. New York: Puffin Books.

Staples, S.F. 1989. *Shabanu*. New York: Random House.

Sterling, D. 1954. *Freedom Train, The Story of Harriet Tubman*. Toronto: Scholastic.

Sterling, S. 1992. *My Name Is Seepeetza*. Vancouver, BC: Douglas and McIntyre.

Temple, F. 1992. *A Taste of Salt*. New York: HarperCollins.

Vos, I. 1986. *Anna Is Still Here*. Toronto: Scholastic.

Watkins, Y.K. 1986. *So Far from the Bamboo Grove*. New York: Beach Tree.

Whelan, G. 1992. *Goodbye, Vietnam*. New York: Randam House.

Winthrop, E. 1985. *The Castle in the Attic*. New York: Bantam Doubleday Dell.

Wright, B.R. 1994. *The Ghost of Popcorn Hill*. New York: Scholastic.

Yolen, J. 1988. *The Devil's Arithmetic*. New York: Puffin Books.

Index